Bodily Engagements with Film, Images, and Technology
Somavision

This book builds a new understanding of the body and its relationship to images and technology, using a framework where novel writings of pragmatist somaesthetics and phenomenology meet new research on bodily reactions.

Max Ryynänen gives an overview of the topic by collecting the existing information of our bodies gazing at visual culture and the philosophies supporting these phenomena, and examines the way the gaze and the body come together in our relationship to culture. Themes covered include somatic film; the body in artistic documentation of activist art; body parts (and their mutilation or surgeries) in contemporary art and film; robot cars and our visual relationship to them; the usefulness of Indian rass philosophy in explaining digital culture; and an examination of Mario Perniola's work about the idea that we, human beings, are increasingly experiencing ourselves to be simply "things."

The book will be of interest to scholars working in art history, aesthetics, cultural philosophy, film studies, technology studies, media studies, cultural studies, and visual studies.

Max Ryynänen is Senior Lecturer of Theory of Visual Culture at Aalto University.

Routledge Focus on Art History and Visual Studies

Routledge Focus on Art History and Visual Studies presents short-form books on varied topics within the fields of art history and visual studies.

Robert Motherwell, Abstraction, and Philosophy
Robert Hobbs

Jimmie Durham, Europe, and the Art of Relations
Andrea Feeser

World-Forming and Contemporary Art
Jessica Holtaway

The Power and Fluidity of Girlhood in Henry Darger's Art
Leisa Rundquist

Buckminster Fuller's World Game and Its Legacy
Timothy Stott

Post-Digital Letterpress Printing
Research, Education and Practice
Edited by Pedro Manuel Reis Amado, Ana Catarina Silva and Vítor Quelhas

Bodily Engagements with Film, Images, and Technology
Somavision
Max Ryynänen

For more information about this series, please visit: https://www.routledge.com/Routledge-Focus-on-Art-History-and-Visual-Studies/book-series/FOCUSAH

Bodily Engagements with Film, Images, and Technology
Somavision

Max Ryynänen

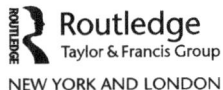

Routledge
Taylor & Francis Group

NEW YORK AND LONDON

First published 2022
by Routledge
605 Third Avenue, New York, NY 10158

and by Routledge
4 Park Square, Milton Park, Abingdon, Oxon, OX14 4RN

Routledge is an imprint of the Taylor & Francis Group, an informa business

Library of Congress Cataloguing-in-Publication Data
Names: Ryynänen, Max, author.
Title: Bodily engagements with film, images, and technology : somavision / Max Ryynänen.
Description: New York : Routledge, 2022. | Includes bibliographical references and index.
Identifiers: LCCN 2022000650 (print) | LCCN 2022000651 (ebook) | ISBN 9781032164281 (hardback) | ISBN 9781032164304 (paperback) | ISBN 9781003248514 (ebook)
Subjects: LCSH: Aesthetics--Physiological aspects. | Human body (Philosophy)
Classification: LCC BH301.P45 R99 2022 (print) | LCC BH301.P45 (ebook) | DDC 111/.85--dc23/eng/20220126
LC record available at https://lccn.loc.gov/2022000650
LC ebook record available at https://lccn.loc.gov/2022000651

ISBN: 978-1-032-16428-1 (hbk)
ISBN: 978-1-032-16430-4 (pbk)
ISBN: 978-1-003-24851-4 (ebk)

DOI: 10.4324/9781003248514

Typeset in Times New Roman
by MPS Limited, Dehradun

Contents

Preface

If someone really ought to be thanked for pushing me to write this book, it would be our dog Ruska, who really made me think about my *reactions* to moving images. Her attacks on (even animated) people and animals on TV forced us to lift the television higher, so that she could not reach it. She made me think that I am sometimes just a scared or defensive mammal when I watch movies.

However, also numerous human scholars, artists, and friends have supported, stimulated and/or criticized me and/or parts of the text, and so helped to forge my work. I am not able to thank everyone who has left a trace in the book, but I want to express my gratitude to at least to some of the people who have done it.

Thank you Richard Shusterman, Riitta Hari, Laura Beloff, Falk Heinrich, Mikko Keskinen, Jozef Kovalcik, Adam Andrzejewski, Heidi Kosonen, Susanne Ylönen, Petteri Enroth, Mike Watson, and Petteri Kummala, who all have commented on the ideas expressed in this book on various occasions. Thank you also Arto Haapala, Danai Anagnostou, Martin Boszorad, Michaela Pastekova, Zoltan Somhegyi, Yvonne Förster, Kevin Tavin, Mira Kallio-Tavin, Mateusz Salwa, Pauline von Bonsdorff, Susanna Välimäki, Juha Torvinen, Liat Grayver, Ossi Naukkarinen, Oiva Kuisma, Sanna Lehtinen, Saara Tuusa, André Maury, Pauli Pylkkö, and Laura Beloff – without forgetting all my colleagues in ViCCA (Aalto ARTS) – for being great teachers, colleagues, and critics. You all have left a trace here.

My deepest gratitude, of course, goes to my family – Riikka Perälä, Jasvitha Ryynänen, Simo Konkka, and my parents Esko Ryynänen and Barbro Wigell-Ryynänen. I would feel cold in this world if you would not exist.

Puotila, (East) Helsinki December 15, 2021

1 Somatic Film: Background, Classification, Education

What is somatic film? Think of all the films that you watch so that your body is actively present, not only the romantic films that warm your heart. Think of your bodily presence during films that raise the hair on the back of your neck, send chills down your spine, make the soles of your feet itch, and/or make you jump out of your chair.

I am interested in our *bodies watching film* (the eye is also part of the body, as much as the brain, of course) – and the way in which the film industry targets it, which has been far more witty than film studies or film criticism in understanding the central nature of the body in film reception. This is not to say that film studies haven't noticed that people who watch movies have a body (although sometimes it feels like it), but the body is still peripheral when film is discussed, a bit like a thing of people interested in body philosophy. It does not do justice to its real presence.

I will delve into different examples to clarify some of the basic aspects of physicality in film viewing, while also discussing the background of our strong reactions to film, for which we human beings have to thank our mammal brains (*Background*). I will discuss somatic film as a category of its own which, partly due to the strong somatic development of film lately, one can start to see as something that differentiates it from other types of films (*Classification*). Although all films have something somatic about them, the somatic side of films is sometimes central, and there is no reason to believe that viewers would not (at least often) realize that they consume these films with their body. I will discuss somatic film history not extensively, but enough, I hope, to make the point that somatic film has been around for a while, and that the concept is needed. I will also inquire into the learning processes at stake. When we watch films, we learn about our bodies, about what we feel is disgusting, for example, and about our boundaries, from (our fear of) death to our reflections on what it might feel

DOI: 10.4324/9781003248514-1

like to lose a limb (*Education*). I see this as something that could be connected to, for example, Stoic philosophical practice, where the search for one's mind–body boundaries was a key to understanding the self. Is it possible to think that the (Greek and Roman) Stoic philosophers gave us a preliminary framework for discussing somatic film? One could also think of the care of the self as proposed by the same Stoics and later discussed by major contemporary thinkers such as Michel Foucault and Richard Shusterman as something that has could help us frame somatic film viewing.

Background

Once or twice a week, while watching a film or TV series, our dog suddenly attacks the screen. I have turned down the volume to test the effect of sound on her, but she continues to attack horses, dogs, and other animals – and sometimes a human, like the fire chief in Milos Forman's *The Firemen's Ball* (1967).

A dog's breed may influence its reactions to TV. Hounds, whose olfactory sense is stronger than their visual sense, do not react as much to television as herding breeds, such as terriers. Ruska (our dog who we adopted at the age of 3) is a mix between a Jack Russell and Parsons Russell terrier. Sometimes, she checks to see if undesired visitors that she saw on the screen have disappeared behind the TV. She doesn't recognize a horse, dog, or cat on my mobile or my computer screen, but our technically relatively advanced television makes her lose her mind.

In any case, dogs have better visual ability than most of us give them credit for. I often hear the comment that dogs are not able to make sense of TV. However, they are more like us than we think. For example, they are able to recognize their own species by looking at an animal's face, although the visual ability of the approximately 400 breeds of dogs in the world vary considerably.[1]

What is interesting, in the way the dog acts, is that when I raise my voice (too often angrily) and say "get away from there," she often does it. This would be a sheer impossibility with a horse, cat, or another dog somewhere in "real life" while walking outside. Doesn't she take the animals on TV seriously?

During a film where there are many of these encounters, and, importantly, many of my negative reactions, she often goes to her own basket and turns around to avoid seeing the moving images. She seems to have some kind of control over her aggression towards these film animals, something lacking in real life when we meet rabbits or squirrels outside our home. It isn't that she would *understand* that the animals on TV are not real, but they definitely do not seem to be in the same category as "real" animals, partly, and I am just guessing here – because they never come off from the screen. To quote animal behaviorist Nicholas Dodman, some dogs "have been desensitized to television. When they see a dog [on TV], they [may] think, 'Those guys just hanging out on the television. They never actually walk around.'"[2]

Increasingly, I feel that my reactions to the manipulations of a film are not much different from those of my dog. Sometimes, they are about the nearly magical make-believe world of fiction. Kendall Walton's classical text on make-believe discusses the way "the barrier" separating our sense of the real world and the fictional one "appears" in some cases "to be psychologically transparent."[3]

Charles is watching a horror movie about a terrible green slime. He cringes in his seat as the slime oozes slowly but relentlessly over the earth destroying everything in its path. Soon a greasy emerges from the undulating mass, and two beady eyes roll around, finally fixing on the camera. The slime, picking up speed, oozed on a new course straight towards the viewers. Charles emits a shriek and clutches desperately at his chair. Afterwards, still shaken, Charles confesses that he was "terrified" of the slime. *Was* he?[4]

Walton's answer is no, but his text spurred reactions by other theorists, some of whom adopted the third view that film audiences are just "irrational, incoherent, and inconsistent" in their relationship to fiction.[5] Some others followed Walton in believing that fear must include a belief that one is in danger and that audiences are so not terrified about what they see on film.[6]

Notes on quasi-emotions (in Walton's case quasi-fear) raise an age-old interest in reactions to fiction, which takes us all the way back to the early theories of aesthetic experience, like Bharata's (500BC–500AD) theory of *rasa*. Rasas, or emotive atmospheres, are based on an idea that was later repeated and philosophically refined on the Indian continent by many thinkers, especially the eleventh century Kashmiri philosopher Abhinavagupta). For the rasa theorists, the emotive effects of theater (fear, love, and hate) are a reflective version of everyday sentiments. The skilled work of the artists absorbs and elevates (real memories of) perceptions and emotions to a higher level into a parallel world, which is based on a higher consciousness, a reflective attitude, which also makes the heightened experience possible (in the original scripts also religiously rewarding). Fear, according to these thinkers, is not fear, but a stunning, reflective version and experience of it.[7] Through the bliss of rasa the audience enters another divine stage of consciousness.

Although I am not convinced that Walton meant it that way, Walton and his "idea of make-believe" have been criticized for our actual lack of choice when facing manipulative fiction. Noël Carroll writes that Walton makes it sound like we could really choose when we enter the mode of make-believe. "I could [so] elect to remain unmoved by *The Exorcist;* I could refuse to pretend I was horrified. But I don't think that was really an option for those, like myself, who were overwhelmingly struck by it."[8]

Sometimes, though, film audiences do not encounter make-believe when they are strongly affected by moving images. Looking at Walton's example, one can ask if it is only fictional make-believe that moves Charles. Even the reader can share Charles' disgusted reaction, to some extent, when trying to understand what Walton is talking about. However, Walton did not explain the narrative context.

To continue on this path of questioning, it might be helpful to look at examples, where we can see a film's physicality at stake without the disturbance of narrative, fictional world-making.

The slime in Walton's example is not just a work of fiction for us. Like Ruska, my dog, we are mammals that react to *seeing* things, of course, without forgetting the strong role of music and sound effects such as in horror movie experiences. We see a slime *moving*. Maybe we even hear the noise it makes as it oozes. Some (like Carroll[9]) think that monsters are popular because we want to learn about them (I have no objections to this); but their victorious presence in film is at least partly about something more than curiosity for the unknown, as their hair-raising impact is so dominant, when we see them. At the moment, when we have been well scared, I don't believe we are experiencing a desire to know more about monsters. We might rather feel like escaping.

In my body philosophy talks, I have used an example from the stunning Tamil film industry, a clip from the 2010 movie *Endhiran,* directed by S. Shankar, and starring Rajinikanth. It perfectly shows film's special quality as somatic stimulation. Although most of my listeners are not from India or that part of the world (e.g. Iran, South East Asia) where Kollywood (in Chennai, the Tamil film industry; or Bollywood, the Mumbai film industry, Lollywood (Lahore), etc.) films land in the mainstream, which means that the cinematic "language" does not appear "natural" to "read," the action still appeals to the viewer somatically.

In the clip, Chitti, a robot played by superstar Rajinikanth, saves a woman, jumps on fast-driving cars, uses multiple guns at the same time, and is so invincible that some viewers might laugh a bit. The clip is 2 or 3 minutes of action. It is absolutely unrealistic, yet comprehensible for anyone, regardless of their prejudices, and stimulating to watch. One sees Chitti, for example, stopping a car with his hands (one can hear the bump), trucks crashing, and bullets going through metal and Chitti himself.

Afterwards, I ask about the audience's bodily reactions to the film, although this is not necessary, as I see people reacting with their feet, rapidly moving their heads, and becoming physically intense during the screening. Not much make-believe about a physical world is constructed, as the clip is so short.

One could, of course, do this even more stoically from an aesthetic point of view, and show just 5 seconds from one of the most vicious punches in the face in Martin Scorsese's *The Raging Bull* (1980) or a scene from any horror or gore movie where someone's skin is cut.[10] It is our relationship to the *seen* that makes movies so effective in a way that is different from other arts.

Current brain research leads us to understand the background for this and other bodily issues involved in watching film. In "Modily Map of Emotions," Lauri Nummenmaa, Enrico Glerean, Riitta Hari, and Jari K. Hietanen report on their tests with film audiences in Finland, Sweden, and Taiwan, in search for emotional "somatosensations" from reactions to the seen and show that they can be mapped quite accurately. Feelings of love were expressed in the chest area, anxiety in the stomach, and shame, besides these places, in the head.[11] We have to thank the somatosensory receptors that are spread around our body and that become activated in different situations, when we think of our abilities of coping with the environment and its many challenges,[12] and the way we observe the complex web of sensational impulses we encounter in everyday life. While watching film, the way in which the areas of the brain that support certain functions in the observer become activated when we see another person's actions and feelings of the same type, is what keeps our bodies intense when we watch even a short silent clip of something that *touches* us.

The mirror neurons of humans as well as monkeys are the base for our emphatic relationship to the seen. This explains many things in our relationship to moving images. One of the strongest most central things we react to is when somebody grabs something.

This is where Vittorio Gallese, Michele Guerra, and Frances Anderson land in their *The Emphatic Screen: Cinema and Neuroscience*.

They ask why movies fascinate us and how they "engage" us.[13] The answer is the liberated embodied simulation that film is, and that actually makes it so different from other arts. Close-ups increase our desire to "reach out and actually touch the image."[14]

Gallese, Guerra, and Anderson write about mirror neurons:

> The discovery of mirror neurons in the brain of the macaque, followed by that of mirroring mechanisms in the human brain [...] has shown that there is a neurobiological foundation for a direct modality of access to the meaning of the behavior and experiences of others. This direct access is independent of the explicit attribution of propositional attitudes such as desires, beliefs, and intentions that are typical of classic cognitivism's standard notion of intersubjectivity. Intersubjectivity is not completely covered in the linguistic-inferential mechanisms of the so-called "Theory of Mind." [...] The discovery of the mirror mechanism in both animal (birds and non-human primates) and human brains opens a new evolutionary scenario that acknowledges "motor cognition" as a cardinal element for the appearance of human intersubjectivity. We do not necessarily need to metarepresent the purposes and motor intentions of others in linguistic form in order to understand them. Most of the time we do not explicitly attribute intentions of others; simply we just understand them. When we are present while others are doing something, we immediately comprehend most of their sensory-motor and emotional intentions without the need to explicitly represent them linguistically.[15]

And, we are "present" in situations we view on film, as our eyes and bodies are not "aware" that we are only watching a film. Mirror neurons activate us both when we execute a motoric action, for example, grab a hammer, and when we just gaze at someone else doing it.

The way we reach "a certain degree of comprehension," as Gallese, Guerra, and Anderson put it,[16] is totally visual, and so it is natural, really *natural*, that the slime "scares" Charles in Walton's example, and that it would maybe scare him even without the film as a whole as a context, with the broader narration. This system described here is also so natural that we create empathy for the characters in the film, as this is one of the functions of the mirroring mechanism.[17]

Gallese, Guerra, and Anderson trace the historical theoretical approaches from Robert Vischer's dichotomy of seeing and active looking (already Winckelmann actually proposed that in addition to just looking, there was a more physically "touching" way to gaze at sculptures[18]) to Aby Warburg.[19] They note how quickly filmmakers learned to achieve an impact on the bodies of the spectators, and how we are not much different from monkeys and apes that share our visual neuroanatomy, as Asif Ghazanfar and Stephen Shepherd show in their study.[20] They present a new take on cinema and the neologisms of "neurofilmology," "neurocinematics," "psychocinematics," and "evolutionary cinematics,"[21] which I truly welcome.

This accent on the brain–body system shares the same aesthetic accent that characterizes works such as Vivian Sobchack's *Carnal Thoughts: Embodiment and Moving Image Culture* (2004), where Jane Campion's *The Piano* (1993) takes on a rather suspect central role (although in Sobchack's work brain research does not yet explain reactions). Chapter 3 of Sobchack's *Carnal Thoughts*, "What My Fingers Knew?" features the tactile reactions and bodily responses that viewers have to the film, from the way the sensitive fingers of the protagonist are presented (especially when she plays the piano) and the horrifying way in which one is chopped off, where we feel an itch in our own fingers.[22]

Interestingly, Sobchack, who otherwise boldly focuses on the body, cannot break ties with the "highbrow" which I think *The Piano* represents, both in bourgeois fashion and by gaining respect on the art scene. Why then choose *The Piano*? And, why do Gallese, Guerra, and Anderson focus so much on directors like Ingmar Bergman? As most highbrow films are so much less physical, one could even ask, as scholars, are they seriously after the body in the film, or are they interested in having a salon chat with highbrow film theorists about "art film," with an accent on the body? Of course, for example Torben Grodal is right in claiming that Alain "Resnais's *Last Year in Marienbad* violated basic emotional and cognitive schemas" through its experimentality that had to do with modes of representation,[23] and this surely created some of its bodily buzz too, but *The Piano* and Bergman's films raise more than the question of whether some people (like Gallese, Guerra, Anderson, and Sobchach) are overtly focused and oversensitized when they watch films that they consider to be somehow monumental, "art" or "culturally significant."

I cannot come up with any other reason than the classical cultural hierarchy proposed by the originally (Western) Central European system of art (later more broadly European and then Global) that then in the end also became the home for highbrow film, a system that conquered the world and overshadowed many other cultural systems.[24] Thinking of the way our bodies are stimulated by even mainstream popular action, horror, and semi-pornographic cinema, this choice renders their ideas with unnecessary categorical weakness. Film as popular culture is the "avant-garde" of somatic film. One can, of course, guess that the reason might lie in the training of these scholars, who might, following arthouse traditions (and more broadly the Western art tradition), accentuate the cognitive side and the aesthetics of the film to the extent that the main focus, the body, becomes overshadowed even in the hunt for good examples for research on somatic film.

I can better understand how Laura Marks, in *The Skin of the Film: Intercultural Cinema, Embodiment, and the Senses* focuses on the way "tactile epistemology" and "embodied perception" bind the viewer to the viewed world.[25] Stressing the haptic over the visual might be one of the key features in connecting worlds and discussing memories, places, and displacement in the works of the Black Audio Film Collective and Trinh T. Minh-ha, among others. Marks shows the importance of sensuality, what she calls "tactile images" in cultural reflection, memories, and intercultural dialogue. This is one meaningful standpoint. She discusses a certain way of doing political art film and the way its somatic sides are needed for its effect. There are no claims about an overall interest in how things work for the mind, body, and/or body–mind. Here art house film has a meaningful role, which is not the case for Gallese, Guerra, Anderson, and Sobchach.

Turning to the meta discussion about the body and film, I feel that first of all, what is still somehow lacking is the observation that some films have really made a cultural tradition out of body stimulation, and, secondly, that after more than 100 years of film we really maybe even should now finally come up with a classification for "somatic film." Although all film has some somatic effects, I would rather reserve this category for the films that base their effectiveness on strong bodily reactions, like itching, jumping, skin orgasms, or disgust, to the extent that the film would not really work without them.

Of course, credit is also due to experimental film. One should not forget that Jan Švankmajer worked with Czech surrealists on film from a tactile point of view. In particular, his famous adaption of Edgar Allan Poe's *The Fall of the House of Usher* (*Zánik dom/Usher,* 1980) includes textures that he hoped to stimulate the viewer somatically (and they do, at least to some extent). (Point for Gallese, Guerra, and Anderson, who mention this.[26]) The strange muddy forms in the work testify to the experimental spirit of the Prague scene at the time.

Still, the arrival of the train in Louis Lumiére's *L'arrivee d'un train a La Ciotat* (*The arrival of the train at La Ciotat*, 1895), which must have felt very physical at the time, to the chills-down-the-spine created by Masaki Kobayashi's *Kwaidan* (1964), there is a difference that is not hard to recognize from the physical reactions one gets from watching Yen Woo-ping's Jackie Chan kung fu film *Drunken Master* (1978), where the protagonist is endlessly kicked and hit in such a *woodywoodpeckerish* and *bugsbunnyesque* manner that our bodies have a hard time coping with it tactilely. The same goes for horror films where slime crawls on skin and bodies are mutilated. In the last examples, the body itself is really the mechanism that supports the film. It is entertainment with our bodies at the center of the enterprise.

It is actually quite perplexing, if one thinks that art house films have grabbed such a big chunk of our discussion of film and the body, but of course, all in all, the body is still too much on a periphery in film discourse. What I find most intriguing is the way one cannot really escape the body's presence in the consumption of film.

My body felt a bit mixed-up following the blood ballet played out in John Woo's *Hardboiled* (1992), and I might have jumped out of my chair once or twice, at least my head did some fast turns when the protagonist, played by Chow Jun-fat, threw a hot pot of tea at a group of Triad members, and when he saved a baby from a burning house. And, I felt an itch, as I watched the staged danger faced by the infant. I had the same reaction when he climbed down, as the camera nicely showed both the height and the way his hands nearly slipped from the rope. In *Mission: Impossible – Ghost Protocol* (2011), it is somatically very stimulating to watch Ethan Hunt (played by Tom Cruise) climb on the impressive windows of Burj Khalifa (828 metres) in Dubai (United Arab Emirates). This scene was so strong that when I visited Dubai I could still feel an echo of this itch in the soles of my feet when I looked at the skyscraper from the ground.

This does not mean that art house classics do not touch our bodies, and I want to accentuate that I am in no way criticizing Sobchack, Gallese, Guerra, or Anderson for their work on, for example, *The Piano* in any other way than that the focus was too much on art film to really, truly build the point of the presence of brain and body in the filmic experience. Art house classics *touch* me as much as they touch them.

Heaviness, of course, really overwhelms me when I watch (one of my favourite films, i.e.) Ingmar Bergman's *Smultronstället* (*Wild Strawberries*, 1957). It produces anxiety that marinates my whole body during the film. An old academic (this is, of course, my not-so-distant future), remembers during a long, anxiety-driven car ride through Sweden (which is my second home country), his not so simple and easy youth, and the web of problems that he had with his partner, who, he realizes, finally, was very, very important for him – too important to lose. It is a long and emotionally complicated filmic story to watch – also for my body. The protagonist recalls and reflects on his failures in life, while facing growing senescence. The film also takes a poetic attitude towards the Swedish language; Bergman is more of a poet than his viewers might have so far understood, and at times this makes me feel physically uncomfortable, as also the words cut deep.

Hardboiled and *Mission: Impossible – Ghost Protocol* are not about the same thing, although one might like to label them just as films like Bergman's. Films they are, of course, but from a somatic point of view, these entertainment films come closer to our amusement park experiences than the European highbrow tradition of painting and literature that Bergman embraces and adapts into film. They are more about instant somatic reactions. Woo's and Brad Bird's films exemplify the way commercial feature films build on somatic stimulation to a much greater extent than most art house films. It is not just that they are full of witty choreographic thinking (if one wants to find a highbrow connection, it would be dance that here comes close to them, not classical theatre) and that the use of camera and the effect production is executed with great skill. You could change a lot in them, from romance to the countries and buildings visited (and destroyed) but you could not take away the dynamic physicality and the action-driven shock-effects, as these features are at the very center of why people watch these films. As our bodies react actively to all filmic violence, one could ask if somatic reactions to film are actually the base also for the pleasure the viewer gains from violence on screen. People tend to discuss only critically film violence, but maybe the way the viewer is at times both the beater and the victim, and the way we so reflect on both sides of the action, while extending our empathy, might be one of the keys for understanding the role of violence in film experience.

If immediate somatic stimulation is commonplace in contemporary film, one wonders whether the audience knows consciously when it seeks for it? It is impossible to prove, but watching people being excited when they go into the movie theater, where the presence of both sound and image is strong and intense, and how happy they are about moments when they jump out of their chairs, makes me feel that if they were qualitatively interviewed, they'd buy my intuition that consuming somatic film is often conscious and that they enter the cinema even mainly for somatic reasons.

Both of the films mentioned, would be easy targets for the classical cultural critic, whom I'd rather call a (Weimarian) cynic (in Peter Sloterdijk's footsteps[27]) who cannot see the value in "other cultures" like the lowbrow (that s/he in some form consumes himself/herself too, if nothing else, through trashy chocolate or any art form where s/he is not a connoisseur). They too often think that entertainment provides an object and/or a tool for passive consumption.[28] If one thinks of James Joyce's *Ulysses* – which I partly enjoy intellectually and re-read some parts like "oh, yes, here he experiments with X," understanding the historical situation in which it was written – or, to take a film example, Alan Resnais's *L'Année dernière à Marienbad* (Last Year at Marienbad, 1961), an intellectual-reflective odyssey, where cracks in the cinematic language are a big deal, as models of *active viewing* (and reading), then I suppose it is understandable that one thinks of more somatic films that activate us through the body, as *passive*. However, it is by no means a sincere way of discussing movies of the type I have mentioned, and it is not fair to choose only one criteria for active/passive. Why not also talk about active/passive in a somatic way?

The active viewer is very much an active body in films like Quentin Tarantino's *Kill Bill* (2003) (which is too often viewed as nothing more than an intertextual game), in *Ichi the Killer* (2001) by Takashi Miike or Johnny To's triad films that significantly change both the rhythm (from meditative – triad bosses talking and eating – to very fast and surprising action, thus producing a shock to the body) and experientially pierce the body of the viewer through raw violence. I wouldn't say that these films are for everyone or that everyone should watch them (but I also wouldn't say that about Bergman or *The Piano*, although I really like them), but these are somatic films par excellence.

The somatically excessive moments of this type of film also provide us with the possibility to reflect on our own physical boundaries (death, pain, loss of limbs) and thus stimulate reflectivity in our bodies, thinking through the body (to borrow Richard Shusterman's expression). Even more: they become present in our bodies, intensively during the film – and sometimes after. I recall my experience of the Burj Khalifa, and how that affected my real encounter with the building, but also, anyone who watches a couple of Charlie Chaplin films in a row cannot escape the way slapstick takes a small hold on how reality is viewed, at least a moment after the films. For example, when one sees a banana, after a Chaplin film, it becomes something that one might slip on.

Much of the success of film is surely based on the viewer's desire to become somatically shaken up. And, as I already expressed, I don't think all the billions of moments when someone went to the movie theater (or turned Netflix on) to see a *body shaker* would just be about non-conscious bodily involvement.

Classification

In "Musical Frisson" (2000)[29] a witty article on the body and listening to music, Jerrold Levinson uses a term with a French origin, "frisson," which translates into "chills" in English,[30] and applies it to musical aesthetics in a way that truly relates to what we discussed in part 1.1. He is interested in somatic reactions to music. Levinson's main question concerns the role and meaning of somatic reactions to our encounters with music, and in a way that I think is useful to pick up here. Traditionally, at least Western intellectuals and academics have not yet really viewed them as very important, but it is good to note that film is not alone in its relative lack of the presence of the body in theoretical discourse.

Most of us have experienced waves of pleasure on the skin. These experiences are sometimes called "skin orgasms," and also Linda Williams mentions them in her classical film study "Film Bodies: Gender, Genre, and Excess" (1991).[31] Levinson brings up certain works of mainstream European and/or Western music where skin orgasms are typical for the reception. One "classical" piece of music that sends chills down the spine is Brahms's *String Quintet in G op. 111*; another better known by a much larger group of bodies, is *The Final Cut* by the British progressive rock band Pink Floyd.[32] Levinson's text is a beautiful call to think about the body in music, and while reading it, I remembered my bodily experience of *The Wall* (1979; another Pink Floyd work).

When one thinks of it, the music of the wealthy and educated (Western) Central European upper class of the early modern period that many of us are accustomed to call classical music, or the British pop tradition, might not even be the strongest contenders for somatic music. Soma can be more central in other traditions, and even more a conscious practice. At least, my spine radiates and the hair on my skin raises when I listen, especially at high volume, to Carnatic (South Indian) music, such as (the contested modernizer) T.M. Krishna's music. The hypnotic drumming that mixes with high-pitched, sometimes excessively extended tones, have a great effect on my body; the organically living/beating drums cast a greater spell when I hear this type of music live. The Japanese "lute," the *biwa*, also has an uncanny impact on me, and it easily fibrillates by back. Traditional Japanese music has played an effective role in the film industry, partly due to the reflective cultural traditionalism of some of the film makers of the 1960s, in particular, Masaki Kobayashi and his film *Kwaidan* (1964), which is just one in a long list of reflectively traditionalist films on the history of Japan, spiced up with philosophical and social perspectives.

Kwaidan is one of my favorite films. But it took a long time before I realized why. One of its (alluringly) disturbing elements is its careful, museum-like following of another, already passed cultural reality, a traditional Japanese one, and the way in which the visually weird sides for the modern (wo)man, from the blackened teeth of upper class women to the lighting of the traditional cities[33] (something Kobayashi and his crew also work on in *Harakiri* (1962)) are presented. One of the main manipulation tools (I am thinking of the aesthetic manipulation of the viewer) in the films is the use of classical Japanese instruments. Both in a filmic, more exegetic way, and in a modernizing way, Toru Takemitsu, who we have to thank for the music, is a real master. Ghosts and uncanny situations (they became so common after this film that they basically created an entire genre) were portrayed auditorially with the help of Japanese classical instruments, and often, the instrument which by itself somehow stimulates my spine, is the *biwa*. The audio track of the dreadful section on *Dan No Ura*, a true historical battle (1185) between the Minamoto and Taira clans, which is the origin of many of the ghosts in the film, is comprised of traditional Japanese music, and really pinches my body. It produces a kind of a semi-violent pleasure, like the scratching of rap records did in the 1990s, while at the same time, hand in hand with the sometimes surprising, but most of the time just intensifying images, it works to dramatize and intensify the entiring experiencing human being, body and mind together, body–mind.

Music that raises hysterical reactions in the audience (strings, or the type of growing or deceasing use of cymbals, which is used by composers like Krystof Penderecky and Kaija Saariaho) and the use of "too low" and somehow abject-driven low sounds are central methods for film-makers and film-composers. The role of music can be more central in cinematic storytelling than what film fans have so far realized.[34] Some horror films without sounds do not work at all.[35]

When films stimulate, control, and/or challenge our bodies, the mind is not very free for intellectual play. As highbrow has with force distanced itself from everything intellectually "easy," and mostly worked at least traditionally by keeping its distance from the "lower senses" and has stressed reflectivity more than "aggressive" stimulation, it is not hard to understand that the body and its role is one of the things that easily functions as (one) divider (among many) for high and low when applied to film or music.

It is also useful to remember that when other forms of stimulation are and have been discussed, our bodies can be approached in a variety of other ways artistically. They can be stimulated by telling stories, beauty/ugliness, and/or narrative suspense (a feature we started with). Rude words can make some viewers blush, even more when one watches films with parents. And, the narrative, when drawing people in, can make the stomach muscles so tense that it can feel like a workout, and in the end when the excitement has been solved, it calls to mind the last minutes of a soccer or hockey match.

Walter Benjamin drew a parallel between hectic factory work, amusement parks, and shock-driven film.[36] The new "art form" of the 1930s became more than just a part of not the entertainment industry and art scenes; it transmitted a tradition that gurus, shamans, and tricksters had worked on for ages, a tradition that worked on taking our breath away and affecting us holistically through illusion. Culture has a long and broad history of somatic takes. Think of dancing to the energetic drumming in Tansanian or Nigerian musical forms. Some of the thoughts that Benjamin had on film's "new" (through fast pace and action) shocking way of touching us might not have been that new, but a reminiscence of the older popular culture traditions and shock conventions that men with Benjamin's stature did not encounter (at least as "culture") before film – like street theater in Naples (for sure an inspiration for Totò and probably a historical background to some of the Marx Brothers slapsticks), Punch and Judy, and circus. But, even in sculpture, it is not always about just form and/or ideas. Here, we can think about Ernst Barlach's statues, which Martin Heidegger mentions when he discusses the presence of *stone* in sculpture, that sensually and materially uncovers our world.[37] or any other use of material in sculpture or architecture that reveals the nature of the material (e.g. Gaudi), sculpture sometimes has a very somatic presence. Film has in a very fresh way come up with new forms of somatic stimulation. And, their presence in our everyday life is surprisingly dominant if one thinks about it. Sculpture might have stimulated us somatically and occasionally has there been circus in town, but now some people engage with somatic film nearly every evening.

Many films are like workouts and they might even, in the end, affect our diet: we do not feel like eating certain things after extreme gore and/or horror films. Some films that we see in the movie theatre cause vertigo. *Spider-Man 3*, where we are swung through a vertically extended city on strings at high speed with the protagonist is a good example of this type of somatic audience manipulation. I recall feeling even a bit dizzy when I came out from the film theatre after seeing it.[38]

After all this, does it not sound reasonable to say that there are somatic films, and not just that there are films that stimulate us somatically, but that there are many of them, and it is a tradition already, a cluster of conventions that we might not have studied as a whole, something that could be classified even, as, like already mentioned, "somatic film" – and that this could/should become more acknowledged by us?[39] It's not that I want to overshadow other classifications and/or genres (or whatever ways of making sense of the variety of film we have), but to add one more extra layer to our understanding of film. As much as we have films mixing the high and the low, or comedy and horror, we could claim that some films are both somatic as well as, for example, horror.

The fascinating thing, I think, is that our bodies read films (like my dog) although they have never heard of fiction. (Well, of course, our brain cells have, and this connection, as presented in the beginning, is crucial for the whole enterprise, but that is a different thing.) Somatic film has a long, long history – and a strong presence in every decade of film history, but, of course, even a stronger, dominating presence with today's technical potential and methods. It might just be that we have yet to reach a new level of understanding, considering brain research and body philosophy, but that film itself has just crossed a line that has made us understand what it is ultimately about. Film now is teaching us in unforeseen ways.

One early instance of somatic film, and maybe the first old film that I remember seeing in a very somatic state, in my childhood, is Harold Lloyd's slapstick comedy *Safety Last* (1923). In the film, the character that Lloyd plays hangs in a life-and-death situation from a pointer of what the films calls "the 12-story Bolton building" (which in real life actually was the International Savings Building in Los Angeles California). Chaplin's work has always struck me as very, very physical, and one can count them in the bursts of laughter that his short films produce, besides the incredible, acrobatic dance-like acting. Countless examples show that some parts of films, and some whole films, are really somatic to the extent and that the label looks meaningful to use.

I would still like to set aside romance, laughter, and pornography from the main use of the concept of somatic film. In some sense pornography totally uses the somatic, but it is no longer interesting as a topic, as its make-believe is somewhat on a zero level (it mostly presents everything as if it would be just true and documentation), and its use is different from the way we enter worlds in feature films. Pornography is somatic on such a basic level that the sense of awe we feel in the heights in *Spider-Man 2* (2004) is missing, and it does not really categorize as "film," although in the old days, some directors had aspirations to make real stories out of it. Of course, it represents a large sub-genre, as people consume a lot of pornography, but in essence it is not film, but mostly just pure visual stimulation, and, of course, we might learn by studying its physical effects more closely. Romance and the already discussed narrative suspense also deal with the body, but their effects are not much different from books or other arts. This leaves us with films that aim to make an impact as the main part to be understood so that the classification makes sense.

I mostly enjoy the moments when I live through cinema more with my body than with my "intellect." The Middle Eastern (think of Christianity) and Central/Southern European accent (philosophy, the art system) on the division of the body and the mind has maybe "helped" to keep us unaware of the role of the body in film, but I am sure that most of us have nothing against this framing. One can even wonder how we started to reflect so much on everything else except for the body in the arts and philosophical thinking.

The art system is relatively young. One could say that it didn't take shape until the mid-eighteenth century, and gained maturity close to the mid-nineteenth century. It bound together the aesthetic cultures that upper class Central European males considered to be high class in early modern times[40] and helped people to see that painting and poetry were about the same thing (this, of course, created a broader community of artists and changed the arts, as they suddenly shared aims and an idea of "themselves"). And, important to note, at the time the body was not very much appreciated, but often debased. Also, there was no film.

This added to what John Dewey traced back to the Greeks, the "people" whose written thinking reflected the world view of non-working free males,[41] and the men who did not suffer from having their souls "twisted following physical work," as Aristoteles nails the problem children of culture in his critique of the theater of the slaves.[42] The fun thing about Aristotle is that he says slaves need a different type of theatre as their souls are distorted by physical work, and perhaps this is still echoed in some of the elitist writing on film, where the tastes of the uneducated are often referred to as somehow connected to their different lives, that is, "consumerist" and "passive" and lacking in education.[43]

In *The 7 Lively Arts* (1924) Gilbert Seldes wanted to defend slapstick film, against the slowly emerging highbrowization of film culture, where many films started to look like bourgeois theater plays.[44] For Seldes, film was original and had its own form of entertainment very different from the theatre, partly due to its different nature. He hints at its somatic potential by his focus on slapstick.

Walter Benjamin believed that *Shock*, which employed montages, close-ups, and the artistically anti-theological nature in, for example, film (it was not into praising original works of art, but copying right from the beginning), was a new key concept for understanding the culture "we live in." It formed a threat to the old art culture, with its cult-driven nature.[45] Although Benjamin did not make the body the stage of his text, it is relevant to note, that the factory work in his descriptions as much as in Charles Chaplin's *Modern Times* (1936) had the shocked and ragged body sometimes in focus (this also applies to "fast traffic" that Benjamin writes about[46]). The lack of a major presence of the body in Western philosophical traditions at the time was maybe the only reason for not including it in the reflection. The body needed stimulation that resonated with factory work, intense street life, and traffic – and their daily shocks, Benjamin could have written. Benjamin also claimed that amusement parks were important for the holistic picture of society and its aesthetic needs.[47] He must have thought about the body.

These, of course, form a very important analogy for what we have discussed in relation to somatic film. One goes to the amusement park for physical action. In film, the critical reaction towards the late 1920s talkie was often directed at its much stiffer nature which was evident if one looked at the slapstick comedies that had been around a few years before that.[48] There must have been a feeling of loss in the circles of film enthusiasts in those times, as more and more, slapstick had to give way to verbal recitals and intellectually dramatic scenarios. Of course, it sometimes came back in new forms. Dario Fo writes beautifully about Totò, the Italian clown and actor, who just hijacked many of the physical street theater methods that were typical for classical Neapolitan culture, for his comedy films.[49]

In any case, throughout the history of film, people have suddenly fallen, and buildings have exploded and thrown people around, but the speed of the images and the rhythm of films have become faster. New threats appear once in a while, along with new heights of challenges to our somatic coping, and they make themselves "heard" in the audience. I still remember when the permissible amount of violence in films jumped a level in the 1990s, and how that felt. Now I am trained for far fiercer challenges. With new horror, everyday pornography, and hectic action, we have entered a stage that old viewers of film and moving images would have had a hard time coping with. In this sense it is also important to note that the consumption of pornography or shocking news might change what is possible to deal with in somatic film.

Does this relate to the way we face endless debates, information, and culture about the body in relationship to sport, sex/gender, and food? (This perspective is a key component in the birth and development of the discussion about somaesthetics.) Think of all the diets that surround us, tai chi and yoga, and gyms and Pilates.[50] Jörg Scheller talks even about a bio-aesthetic turn of *entelechy*.[51] Anorexia and body anxiety steer the behavior of the masses.[52] For decades, many of us were not aware of the fact that we had a living body that guided our emotions and thoughts. Now, things have changed. Has the development of somatic film nothing to do with this? Our bodies watch films. They thrive on the chills down the spine. They gain "skin orgasms." They feel itching in their hands and in the soles of their feet. Bodies are being touched, mutilated, hit, and sexually stimulated in film like never before.

One of my favorite classics in cultural theory, Herbert Marcuse's philosophical, but quite hippiesque *An Essay on Liberation* (1969), which is one of the main books steering classical leftist theory into contemporary liberal thinking with its more holistic approach (including race, gender, and popular culture), is full of bodily remarks, just at the advent of alternative cultures and the new rise of the really somatic film that came around at the time (as described earlier). Marcuse, who used to be (and later again became[53]) an advocate of nihilist, cynical intellectualism, where highbrow art and traditional scientific world-views were the last threshold of resistance against easy hedonism and consumerism, appreciated in a slightly a utopian way the new potential of popular culture and its interest in sensuality and sensual practices. He lived in California at this time, and could comment on the early days of the hippie movement, not its stranding in other states and countries through the commercialized distribution of revolutionary "Americana." Marcuse does not mention film, but he writes enthusiastically about sensual music and long hair. Although he did not seem to understand that he was writing really a lot about bodily issues, he believed that these cracks in the Western cultural system (the negative dialectics that he picked up from Theodor Adorno and Max Horkheimer) could have the potential to create the growth of real change.[54] Film could be easily inscribed into Marcuse's work. It had only just made it to a new level somatically, one that changed closer to the millennium. Georges Franju's *Eyes without a Face* (1960) still raises disgust in today's viewers as it shows bizarre and truly disgusting operations. In *Repulsion* (1965), Roman Polanski took the body of ("too") beautiful Catherine Deneuve and her fears/disgusts and made it the focal point for experiencing moving images in a way that shocked audiences at the time. And, finally, George A. Romero's *Night of the Living Dead* (1968) brought living corpses and their violent shock effects into mainstream culture. Perhaps Benjamin, if he'd live in this era, would have walked home and written in his diary: "I felt physically uneasy in the cinema. What's going on?"

The "care of the self" which I think we should consider has some sort of a role here, accompanied these new film practices. The concept was coined by Michel Foucault in his *History of Sexuality*, where somatic practices of self-care entered the modern canon of philosophy and idea history. Foucault was inspired by Greek stoic self-care. When the concept of care of the self is raised, one can quite easily imagine a harmonious new-age scene, maybe something like a hot yoga studio – maybe even a cheesy one, in the worst place. But care can be different, as anyone who has done hard craving sports knows. We use film in various ways. When do you look at horror films? Probably not when you are really tired and feeling fragile emotionally – or when your close friend just died. But there are other moments in which you might want to be shocked, and we change our appetite for culture and its somatic sides following what happens in life. Benjamin thinks that the new art forms were created to resonate with our everyday, but it is often the opposite. I will only watch a fast-paced action film when I'm feeling slow. When I am hyped up by hectic work I take a filmic "downer" – not Marguerite Duras's *India Song* (1975), as it craves focused thinking too (one has to really be in the right mood), but maybe *The Piano*. It is more like: when I have been eating too heavy stuff, I order a salad.

It would be too much trouble (and the wrong context) to work out a taxonomy of somatic film, but it wouldn't be hard to sketch up a list about it: horror, action, disgust, and nausea are tags that relate to straight sexual stimulation, and feelings of fear, shocks like jumping out of the chair, reactions of disgust and dizziness, maybe even close to vertigo. One could focus, accordingly, on the sexual organs (such as the nipples or anus), the back and the neck, the feet (ready to run), and the stomach, to make somatically wider our conceptions of aesthetic experience, which even in Dewey's work, where the body's role is accentuated, have no detailed account. At least at some point, if we want to really understand film, we need to somehow work out a detailed taxonomy of its physical effects. Getting back to the Stoics, whom I will soon give a larger role, we need to learn about the way people consciously work to intensify and to stimulate *physis* (φύσις; Greek for nature, with an accent on our natural development, and growth) through film, without forgetting how much professionals in film work on helping them with this.

It is not a coincidence that people in sports have considerably greater bodily self-consciousness. I love reading *Sports Illustrated*. The authors are well aware of the bodily tensions of whatever practice they cover from rest to warming up, or gazing intensely at an ice hockey match. They write about how watching sport relieves tensions when there are fights and goals (and they use words like "cathartic" to describe this).

Since movie critics do not usually write about somatic reactions, they could learn from sports journalists. Vivian Sobchack notes this[55] and I just don't understand why she can find this in sport but not really step into the world of a somatic popular film (I still owe this to her). The feeling when a really good thriller, like *The Rear Window* (1954) massages our stomachs might actually connect to our reactions to a game – like mine during a Finland vs. Canada ice hockey match.

Alfred Hitchcock's *Rear Window* is in many ways an interesting movie somatically. A man sitting in a wheelchair, a good analogy of the viewer who sits without any possibility to move "in the film" and help people in distress, witnesses a ruthless murder. The killer realizes that his act has not gone unseen. The bodily tensions that follow, based on narrative make-believe, good close-ups, and intensifying music (by Franz Waxman and Leonard Bernstein) follow this in a way that makes the viewer troubled intellectually (did he ...? will he ...?) but also somatically.

Rear Window proceeds through our fostered empathy for the protagonist and stimulates us in a traditionally artistic way, using extremely effective narrative suspense both textually (the manuscript, the discussions) and visually (the close-ups and changing perspectives). It is a great example of a suspense-based somatic film. It does not impose on us nearly anything through reactions like disgust or strong imagery.

Thrillers are physical but they often lack the immediate somatic

stimulation of the types discussed earlier, although we become surprised once or twice with a hand wielding a knife or something similar.
It is different from what I'd call *shock-based somatic film*. Some
horror-films that "negatively" surprise the audience belong to this
category. There is, of course, a difference in surprising people and
testing the limits of what the audience "can take." The famous cutting
of the eye in Luis Bunuel's and Salvador Dali's *An Andalucian Dog*
(1929) was a surrealist strategy to stimulate our unconscious, and even
more, our ideas on it maybe, but today's excessive torture scenes and
bloody, ethically unfair mistreatment of various people that take shape
for example in Takashi Miike's *Ichi the Killer* (2001) or Dario
Argento's *Suspiria* (1977) are about going over the line stimulation-
wise, to make us reach a moment when we feel like "this is it, I've had
enough." The Stoic philosophers who eagerly discussed and practiced
self-care and some sort of self-analysis (not psycho-analysis, though),
constantly dealt with their boundaries. Looking at their work and
practices might help us to find a new twist in the road to understanding
what films, sometimes very somatic ones, are all about.

Education

When discussions about new media erupted in the 1980s and even
more in the 1990s, we often felt perplexed about the effects of media.
The experiences that they provided through their culture were often
more important for the discussion than the technical details they often
worked harder with. In 1995, Derrick de Kerckhove proposed that
new media culture had developed something close to phantom limb
experiences. He wrote that we react to organs or bodily extensions in
film as if they belonged to us.[56] In the beginning of this book, we found
some explanations for this in the parts observing the findings in brain
research. But well, it is said that he too often uses the phantom limb
concept. It is not a bad metaphor, though, as long as one accepts that
it is just an allegorical way to relate to the topic. Interestingly, although he also worked in new media, that was not what advanced
these issues. We are still not sitting with VR helmets on at home, although this was what the media theorists of the 1990s dreamt about.
Even if our domestic tech has developed, we often look at moving
images with less advanced technology visually speaking – from a
laptop screen or even a mobile phone. But, everyday popular culture
and feature films have taken a much more pioneering role somatically.
The masses desire to feel those "phantom limbs" but in more classical
ways, as, for example, members of TV audiences.

For me, Toshiya Fujita's *Lady Snowblood* (1973) offers a quintessential "phantom limb experience," when the protagonist, magically played by Meiko Kaji, cuts off her enemies' hands. Sometimes, as I watch the film, I really feel an itch in my hand when a hand is cut off on the screen. My mind knows that I am watching a film, but some parts of my brain and my hand, the thinking part of my body, live through these losses as if they were part of "real life."

Kevin Tavin and Mira Kallio-Tavin have accentuated the role of excess in learning about ourselves[57] and extreme works of art, in Zhu Yu's *Eating People* (2000), in which where the artist claimed (and actually lied) that he really ate a fetus; in one way or another, they make us confront our boundaries as human beings and thus have some sort of educational value.[58]

This attitude can increasingly be found in contemporary art education.[59] I guess they show another, related position towards the boundaries that the Stoics challenged and that Foucault, among others, wrote about. The early philosophical ideas and practices (philosophy was a philosophy of life then in a major part of Southern Europe, the Middle East, and North Africa) of care of the self were somewhat connected to medical practices. But they sound sporty too. How could one learn to know oneself, to reflect better on oneself (Foucault asks)?[60] The care-system of the Stoics was both research (of oneself and human boundaries all and all) and a kind of a reflective sport, a method of training where philosophical thought and practical ethical praxis met. As a proponent of sadomasochism, Foucault accentuates the excessive training methods mentioned. They had a strong auto-communicative tenet. The aspiration was to grow control, self-control more than anything else. And, to do this, one needed to learn about limits. The mentioned examples take up even absurd situations and practices that today only raise eyebrows. One is found in Plutarch's work[61] where excessive sports exercises are immediately followed by anti-culinary, anti-hedonistic practices, where one asked the slaves (sigh) to prepare a table of delicacies, which was then just gazed upon.

Foucault focuses on the self-reflective power of these practices. *Speculator*, a self-reflective human being, was the aspiration, the focus, and the goal for this sometimes absurd fostering of oneself. According to Foucault, Seneca, the philosopher, applies *excutere* (lat.) to all of these Stoic bodily practices. *Excutere* means shaking or agitating. Aren't these really good words for our use of somatically excessive movies?

No doubt, we occasionally enjoy or learn from testing our boundaries through film. We might want to learn about monsters (as Carroll says), but we also want to learn about ourselves – and in various ways, not just psychoanalytically (this line of thought dominated many studies about horror in the old days) but also somatically. We are a body and we have bodies, as the phenomenologists say, and we note and reflect on the boundaries and the very nature of our bodies through filmic enjoyment, horror, and disgust. Our mindsets, as much as our body-sets, are constantly trained and tested for the still unknown. I have never been in a big fire, but I have some ideas about it that I have gathered from film.[62] The same applies to extreme forms of sex and violence.

We know that people watch movies and television differently. How about their different somatic ways of connecting to somatic film? We need to really, really take up a new aspiration on how to learn more about these practices, from interviewing people to maybe keeping our own bodily film diaries. I recall that the different interpretative strategies presented in John Fiske's *Television Culture* (1988)[63] once stunned me, and I understood how, as an individual and part of different groups of people (Nordic, male, working class), I saw moving images differently from someone else. Who would write the same kind of a book about people's bodies while watching films?

My body is rarely shaken in my non-cinematic everyday life. Of course, there are heights offered by a variety of pleasures, like delicacies. It is not that my life is boring, but I am not chased by violent criminals. I realize, however, that film, together with the gym, sushi, my toilet visits (these are really underrated pleasures) and sex is one way to be holistically alive, the body being sometimes even challenged. Just as moving images are taking a much stronger hold of us than ever before it is hard for us to realize where reality ends and film begins. This is not to rely solely on Baudrillard's idea that too many images make us see the world through a framework created by them,[64] but to remember that even if we are rational animals, our bodies, which are very receptive with the help of our brains, do not know about the distance we emphasize that separates film from what happens on the street and in the bedroom. This should not just touch our ideas on the body–mind, but also the whole idea of (aesthetic) experience. While, for example, John Dewey described well the organic (naturalist) base of our experience of culture, he (as he did not have brain science to work with) lacked an understanding of the way the body is stimulated by culture, and even more, he did not follow his holistic theory of experience, which was supposed to rethink the role of art in human life, to its messy end: films and other images are all over the place, also where we do not expect to find them, in the everyday.

Art educators could find a new niche if they would be ready to train themselves in Feldenkrais, yoga, and/or somaesthetics, to accompany their already existing profession. Yoga teachers help us to understand what happens when we are upside down. Could someone not help other people to understand what happens somatically when they watch film?

Two millennia ago, Seneca wrote that people travel too much, as most things happen inside of us.[65] Practically speaking the same is, of course, written in chapter 47 of the Tao Te Ching, where we are reminded of the need to turn to the soma: "The Master arrives without leaving/sees the light without looking/achieves without doing a thing."[66] Sounds like a good old movie evening with "passivating films"!

Conclusions

Contemporary brain research explains many of our reactions to film. The film industry has produced a whole category of films where these reactions are central. I would like to call this "somatic film." There is no reason to believe that we do not, at least sometimes, choose somatic film for somatic reasons. But films also educate us. We learn about our somatic boundaries. Our attitude towards film has to change if we want to understand somatic film. Too many scholars are looking only at highbrow film, although popular film is much more somatic. We need to look more at popular film to understand the role of the body. More research is also needed, not just on the category, but on the variety of somatic responses we have. The new perspective on film offers, also, a variety of educational and scholarly possibilities.

Notes

1 Dominique Autier-Dérian, Bertrand L. Deputte, Karine Chalvet-Monfray, Marjorie Coulon, and Luc Mounier, "Visual Discrimination of Species of Dogs (Canis familiaris)," *Animal Cognition* 16, no.4 (July 2013): 637–651. See also Liz Langley's interview with Nicholas Dodman on dogs watching TV in *National Geographic,* January 10, 2015. "Why Do Dogs Watch – and React to – TV?" https://www.nationalgeographic.com/news/2015/1/150111-animals-dogs-television-pets-science-tv-behavior/
2 In Langley's interview (see previous footnote).
3 Kendall Walton, "Fearing Fictions," *The Journal of Philosophy* LXXV, no. 1 (January 1978): 5.
4 Ibid.
5 Colin Radford, "Tears and Fiction," *Philosophy* 52 (1997): 208–213.
6 Walton writes: "It seems a principle of common sense, one which ought not to be abandoned if there is any reasonable alternative, that fear must be

accompanied by, or must involve, a belief that one is in danger." Walton, "Fearing Fictions," 6–7. Still, Walton's example shows real reactions, not pretended ones, as Alex Neill nails it in his article "Fear, Fiction and Make-Believe," *The Journal of Aesthetics and Art Criticism* 49, no. 1 (Winter 1991): 47–56.

7 Bharata Muni, *The Nāṭyaśāstra: English Translation with Critical Notes* (New Delhi: Munshiram Manoharlal Publishers, 1984). For Abhinavagupta's more philosophical interpretation of the *rasa*, where the role of the audience is expanded, see Raniero Goli, *The Aesthetic Experience According to Abhinavagupta* (Varanasi: Chowkhamba Sanskrit Series, 1956).

8 Noël Carroll, *The Philosophy of Horror; or, Paradoxes of the Heart* (New York: Routledge, 1990), 74.

9 Carroll, *The Philosophy of Horror*.

10 Especially, in Anglo-American mainstream film, one weird repetitive formula of this type is the rape scene, which makes the viewer react somatically to the unpleasant scenario. On this, see Sarah Projansky, *Watching Rape: Film and Television in Postfeminist Culture* (New York: New York University Press, 2001).

11 Lauri Nummenmaa, Enrico Glenean, Riitta Hari, and Jari K. Hietanen, "Bodily Maps of Emotions," *PNAS* 111, no. 2 (2014): 646–651.

12 For more, see Kaisu Lankinen, Eero Smeds, Pia Tikka, Elina Pihko, Riitta Hari, and Miikka Koskinen, "Haptic Contents of a Movie Dynamically Engage the Spectator's Sensorimotor Cortex," *Human Brain Mapping* 37 (2016): 4061–4068.

13 Vittorio Gallese, Michele Guerra, and Frances Anderson, *The Empathic Screen: Cinema and Neuroscience* (Oxford: Oxford University Press, 2019), viii (Murray Smith's preface).

14 Ibid., xxiii.

15 Ibid., 3–4.

16 Ibid., 5.

17 Ibid.

18 See, for example, Yanping Gao's analysis on what he calls Winckelmann's "haptic gaze": Yanping Gao, "Winckelmann's Haptic Gaze: A Somaesthetic Interpretation," in *Aesthetic Experience and Somaesthetics*, edited by Richard Shusterman, 71–86 (Leiden – Boston: Brill, 2018).

19 Gallese, Guerra, and Anderson, *The Emphatic Screen*, 5–8. For early work on film mentioned by Gallese, Guerra, and Anderson, where physicality is somehow taken up in the aforementioned sense, see, for example, Hugo Münsterberg, *The Photoplay: A Psychological Study* (New York – London: D. Appleton and Company, 1916). Thinking of books that are not mentioned, Ute Holl's, *Cinema, Trance, and Cybernetics* (Berlin: Verlag Brinkmann & Bose, 2002) comes close to the problematics, from time to time. See also Jennifer M. Barker's *Tactile Eye: Touch and the Cinematic Experience* (Berkeley: University of California Press, 2009). Cognitive sciences have lately become increasingly usual partners for art theory and aesthetics. Although not a film book, Giovanni Matteucci's *Estetica e natura umana*, which focuses on expression, discusses in depth the cognitive background for some of the issues that have traditionally been thought about only from the point of view of philosophy and the humanities, and serves as a book aiming to

understand the biological background for aesthetics. Giovanni Matteucci, *Estetica e natura umana* (Roma: Carocci, 2019).

20   Asif Ghazanfar and Stephen Shepherd, "Monkeys at the Movies: What Evolutionary Cinematics Tells Us about Film," *Projections* 5 (2011): 1–25.

21   Ibid., 47.

22   Vivian Sobchack, *Carnal Thoughts: Embodiment and Moving Image Culture* (Berkeley: University of California Press, 2004), 53–84.

23   Torben Grodal, *Embodied Visions: Evolution, Emotion, Culture, and Film* (Oxford: Oxford University Press, 2009), 9. In his "evolutionary bioculturalism," Grodal attempts to synthetize emotions, reactions, and aesthetics in an impressive way.

24   See Max Ryynänen, *On The Philosophy of Central European Art: The History of an Institution and its Global Competitors* (Lanham: Lexington Books (an imprint of Rowman and Littlefield), 2020). See especially chapter 1 for the development of the system. For the "Western" system, which quite naturally became the destiny of quite a lot of film already from the early days of moving image, see also Larry Shiner, *The Invention of Art: A Cultural History* (Chicago and London: The University of Chicago Press, 2001); Władysław Tatarkiewicz, *History of Six Ideas* (Warsaw: Polish Scientific Publishers, 1980); Paul Oskar Kristeller, "The Modern System of the Arts: A Study in the History of Aesthetics," Part I, *Journal of the History of Ideas* 12, no. 4 (October 1951): 496–527; and Lydia Goehr, *Imaginary Museums of Musical Work: An Essay in the Philosophy of Music* (Oxford UK: Oxford University Press, 1992).

25   Laura Marks, *The Skin of the Film: Intercultural Cinema, Embodiment, and the Senses* (Durham and London: Duke University Press, 2000), 138.

26   This historical discourse, by Gallese, Guerra, and Anderson, leads to seeing the history of film in a new way. Gallese, Guerra, and Anderson, *The Emphatic Screen*, 170–172.

27   Sloterdijk (1983) recalls that cynics were actually, in the beginning "barking dogs" (the etymological root of the concept) that did not respect people in power and that opened their mouth about issues that they were not hoped to. Another type of cynicism came up in late-nineteenth century in Weimar (then spread out to the whole Western world), where intellectuals had a more of a nihilist (and I think often unfair) attitude towards (other) culture(s, like entertainment). See *The Critique of Cynical Reason* (London: Verso, 1988).

28   See, for example, Bernard Rosenberg and David M. White, eds., *Mass Culture: The Popular Arts in America* (Glencoe: The Free Press, 1959).

29   Jerrold Levinson, "Musical Frissons," *Revue française d'études américaines*, 86 (2000): 64–76.

30   There is a natural scientific background to Levinson's study. Jaak Panksepp did empirical research work on chills in the 1990s. Jaak Panksepp, "The Emotional Sources of 'Chills' Induced by Music," *Music Perception: An Interdisciplinary Journal* 13, no. 2 (1995): 171–207.

31   Levinson, "Musical Frissons," 65; Linda Williams, "Film Bodies: Gender, Genre, and Excess," *Film Quarterly* 44, no. 4 (Summer 1991): 2–13, note on page 5. Another great take on the excessive physicality in film, which takes up things like this, is Carol J. Clover, "Her Body, Himself: Gender in the

Slasher Film," *Representations*, no. 20, Special Issue: Misogyny, Misandry, and Misanthropy (Autumn, 1987): 187–228.

32 Levinson, "Musical Frissons," 67–69.

33 Here, we echo Junichiro Tanizaki's aesthetics-driven essay *In Praise of Shadows*, where he takes up the role of blackened teeth in the holistic nature of traditional Japanese (although he does not point it out: upper class) culture. Junichiro Tanizaki, *In Praise of Shadows* (Chicago: Leete's Island Books, 1977). See also Hiroshi Yoshioka's "A Cultural Approach to Sex-related Disgust: Rethinking Shunga and other "perversions" in the twenty-first century," in *Cultural Approaches to Disgust and the Visceral*, edited by Max Ryynänen, Heidi Kosonen, and Susanne Ylönen (London – New York: Routledge, forthcoming). Yoshioka discusses the way these blackened teeth look disgusting for contemporary Japanese people.

34 For a great take on the, sometimes even, sneaky role of film music, see Susanna Välimäki, *Miten sota soi? Sotaelokuva, ääni ja musiikki* (Tampere: Tampere University Press, 2008).

35 The support of music is, of course, important to other arts too, for example, dance and music.

36 See Benjamin's notes on, for example, factories and Tivoli in his *Charles Baudelaire: A Lyric Poet in the Era of High Capitalism* (London: Verso, 1997).

37 Martin Heidegger, *The Origin of the Work of Art*, in *Poetry, Language, Thought*, Trans. Albert Hofstadter (New York: Harper & Row, 1975).

38 Thank you Sari Tervaniemi for convincing me to come to the movies to see the film.

39 I have already presented the concept in an earlier, sketchy version of these thoughts, "Sending Chills Up My Spine: Somatic Film and the Care of the Self," in *Art, Excess, and Education: Historical and Discursive Contexts*, edited by Kevin Tavin, Mira Kallio-Tavin, and Max Ryynänen, 83–197 (New York: Palgrave, 2019).

40 See Ryynänen, *On The Philosophy of Central European Art*; Shiner, *The Invention of Art*; Tatarkiewicz, *History of Six Ideas*; Kristeller, "The Modern System of the Arts"; and Goehr, *Imaginary Museums of Musical Works*.

41 John Dewey, *Art as Experience* (New York: Pedigree Books, 1980), chapter 7.

42 Aristotle, *Politics* (Oxford: Oxford University Press, 1999), Book 8: 1342A.

43 Herbert Gans's *Popular Culture and High Culture: An Analysis and Evaluation of Taste* (New York: Basic Books, 1974) is a good example of this type of hierarchical thinking. For more, see the critique of Gans and other critical theorists in Richard Shusterman, *Pragmatist Aesthetics: Living Beauty, Rethinking Art* (London: Blackwell, 1992).

44 Gilbert Seldes, *The 7 Lively Arts* (New York: Harper & Brothers Publishers, 1924), 310–312.

45 Walter Benjamin, "The Work of Art in the Age of its Technological Reproducibility," in *The Work of Art in the Age of its Technological Reproducibility and Other Writings on Media*, edited by M. Jennings, B. Doherty, and T. Levin, 19–55 (Cambridge, MA: The Belknap Press of Harvard University Press, 2008).

46 Benjamin, *Charles Baudelaire*, has Benjamin describing with awe, for example, the fast and fragmented nature of modern traffic, where, for example, signs, lights, and other vehicles that one meets, have a sort of shocking role, which resembles the nature of film.
47 Ibid.
48 Not just Seldes writes about this: look also at Henry Parland's film essays: Henry Parland, *Idealrealisation* (Helsinki: Söderströms, 1929).
49 Dario Fo, *Totò: Manuale dell' attor comico* (Firenze: Vallechi Editore, 1995).
50 See, for example, Richard Shusterman's reflection on this in *Thinking Through the Body* (Cambridge: Cambridge University Press, 2012).
51 Jörg Scheller, *No Sports! Zur Ästhetik des Bodybuildings* (Stuttgart: Franz Steiner Verlag, 2010), 65.
52 Henri Hyvönen, "Care of the Self, Somaesthetics and Men Affected by Eating Disorders: Rethinking the Focus on Men's Beauty Ideals," *The Journal of Somaesthetics* 6, no. 2 (2020): 64–81.
53 Herbert Marcuse, *The Aesthetic Dimension: Towards a Critique of Marxist Aesthetics* (London: MacMillan, 1979).
54 Herbert Marcuse, *An Essay on Liberation* (Boston: Beacon Press, 1969).
55 Sobchack, 2004, 53–54.
56 Derrick de Kerckhove, *The Skin of Culture: Investigating the New Electronic Reality* (London: Kogan Page, 1997).
57 Kevin Tavin and Mira Kallio-Tavin, "The Cat, the Cradle, and the Silver Spoon: Violence in Contemporary Art," *Studies in Art Education: A Journal of Issues and Research* 56, no. 1 (2016): 426–437.
58 For more on the active use of the body in contemporary art in China, see, for example, Hubert Chuan, *The Body at Stake: Experiments in Chinese Contemporary Art and Theatre* (Bielefeld: Transcript Verlag, 2013). The book consists of interviews with contemporary artists.
59 See, for example, Juuso Tervo, "Pedagogical Sacrifices: On the Educational Excess of John Duncan's Darkness," in *Art, Excess, and Education*, edited by Kevin Tavin, Mira Kallio-Tavin, and Max Ryynänen, 129–144.
60 Michel Foucault, *History of Sexuality: The Care of the Self* (Part 3) (New York: Pantheon Books, 1984), 189–210.
61 Ibid.
62 The main problem of big fires in films is, of course, the fact that in real fires one cannot really see much. I owe this point to fire chief Tommi Leppioja.
63 John Fiske, *Television Culture* (London: Methuen, 1988).
64 Jean Baudrillard, *Simulacra and Simulation* (Ann Arbor: University of Michigan Press, 1994).
65 Seneca, *Moral Letter to Lucilius*, letter 104. C. 65. Wikisource: https://en.wikisource.org/wiki/Moral_letters_to_Lucilius/Letter_104.
66 Lao-Tzu, *Tao Te Ching* (New York: Harper Perennial, 1988), 47.

Bibliography

Aristotle. *Politics*, trans. David Keyt. Oxford: Oxford University Press, 1999.
Autier-Dérian, Dominique, Bertrand L. Deputte, Karine Chalvet-Monfray, Marjorie Coulon, and Luc Mounier. "Visual Discrimination of Species of Dogs (Canis familiaris)." *Animal Cognition* 16, no. 4 (July 2013): 637–651.

Barker, Jennifer M. *Tactile Eye: Touch and the Cinematic Experience*. Berkeley: University of California Press, 2009.

Baudrillard, Jean. *Simulacra and Simulation*. Ann Arbor: University of Michigan Press, 1994.

Benjamin, Walter. *Charles Baudelaire: A Lyric Poet in the Era of High Capitalism*. London: Verso, 1997.

Benjamin, Walter. "The Work of Art in the Age of its Technological Reproducibility." In *The Work of Art in the Age of its Technological Reproducibility and Other Writings on Media*, edited by M. Jennings, B. Doherty, and T. Levin, 19–55. Cambridge, MA: The Belknap Press of Harvard University Press, 2008.

Carroll, Noël. *The Philosophy of Horror: or, Paradoxes of the Heart*. New York: Routledge, 1990.

Clover, Carol J. "Her Body, Himself: Gender in the Slasher Film." *Representations* Vol 20, Special Issue: Misogyny, Misandry, and Misanthropy (Autumn, 1987): 187–228.

De Kerckhove, Derrick. *The Skin of Culture: Investigating the New Electronic Reality*. London: Kogan Page, 1997.

Dewey, John. *Art as Experience*. New York: Pedigree Books, 1980.

Fiske, John. *Television Culture*. London: Methuen, 1988.

Fo, Dario. *Totò: Manuale dell' attor comico*. Firenze: Vallechi Editore, 1995.

Foucault, Michel. *History of Sexuality: The Care of the Self* (Part 3). New York: Pantheon Books, 1984.

Gallese, Vittorio, Michele Guerra, and Frances Anderson. *The Empathic Screen: Cinema and Neuroscience*. Oxford: Oxford University Press, 2019.

Gans, Herbert. *Popular Culture and High Culture: An Analysis and Evaluation of Taste*. New York: Basic Books, 1974.

Gao, Yanping. "Winckelmann's Haptic Gaze: A Somaesthetic Interpretation." In *Aesthetic Experience and Somaesthetics*, edited by Richard Shusterman, 71–86. Leiden – Boston: Brill, 2018.

Ghazanfar, Asif, and Stephen Shepherd. "Monkeys at the Movies: What Evolutionary Cinematics Tells Us about Film." *Projections* 5 (2011): 1–25.

Goehr, Lydia. *Imaginary Museums of Musical Work: An Essay in the Philosophy of Music*. Oxford UK: Oxford University Press, 1992.

Grodal, Torben. *Embodied Visions: Evolution, Emotion, Culture, and Film*. Oxford: Oxford University Press, 2009.

Heidegger, Martin. *The Origin of the Work of Art*, in *Poetry, Language, Thought*, trans. Albert Hofstadter. New York: Harper & Row, 1975.

Holl, Ute. *Cinema, Trance, and Cybernetics*. Berlin: Verlag Brinkmann & Bose, 2002.

Hyvönen, Henri. "Care of the Self, Somaesthetics and Men Affected by Eating Disorders: Rethinking the Focus on Men's Beauty Ideals." *The Journal of Somaesthetics* 6, no. 2 (2020): 64–81.

Kate. *The Body and the Screen: Female Subjectivities in Contemporary Women's Cinema*. New York: Bloomsbury, 2017.

Konrad, Eva-Maria, Thomas Petraschka, and Christiana Werner. "The Paradox of Fiction – A Brief Introduction into Recent Developments, Open Questions, and Current Areas of Research, including a Comprehensive Bibliography from 1975 to 2018." *Journal of Literary Theory* 12, no. 2 (2018): 193–203.

Kristeller, Paul Oskar. "The Modern System of the Arts: A Study in the History of Aesthetics." Part I. *Journal of the History of Ideas* 12, no. 4 (October 1951): 496–527.

Langley, Liz. "Why Do Dogs Watch – and React to – TV?" *National Geographic*, January 10, 2015. https://www.nationalgeographic.com/news/2015/1/150111-animals-dogs-television-pets-science-tv-behavior/. Last accessed December 10, 2021.

Lankinen, Kaisu, Eero Smeds, Pia Tikka, Elina Pihko, Riitta Hari, and Miikka Koskinen. "Haptic Contents of a Movie Dynamically Engage the Spectator's Sensorimotor Cortex," *Human Brain Mapping* 37 (2016): 4061–4068.

Lao-Tzu. *Tao Te Ching*. New York: Harper Perennial, 1988.

Levinson, Jerrold. "Musical Frissons." *Revue française d'études américaines* 86 (2000): 64–76.

Matteucci, Giovanni. *Estetica e natura umana*. Roma: Carocci, 2019.

Marcuse, Herbert. *An Essay on Liberation*. Boston: Beacon Press, 1969.

Marcuse, Herbert. *The Aesthetic Dimension: Towards a Critique of Marxist Aesthetics*. London: MacMillan, 1979.

Monod, Jean-Claude. "Why I Talk to My Dog." *Environmental Philosophy* 11, no. 1 (Spring 2014): 17–26.

Marks, Laura. *The Skin of the Film: Intercultural Cinema, Embodiment, and the Senses*. Durham and London: Duke University Press, 2000.

Marx, Karl. *Capital*. London: Penguin Classics, 1990.

Mulvey, Laura. "Visual Pleasure and Narrative Cinema." *Screen* 16, no. 3 (1976): 6–18.

Münsterberg, Hugo. *The Photoplay: A Psychological Study*. New York – London: D. Appleton and Company, 1916.

Neill, Alex. "Fear, Fiction and Make-Believe." *The Journal of Aesthetics and Art Criticism* 49, no. 1 (Winter 1991). 47–56.

Nummenmaa, Lauri, Enrico Glenean, Riitta Hari, and Jari K. Hietanen, "Bodily Maps of Emotions," *PNAS* 111, no. 2 (2014): 646–651.

Panksepp, Jaak. "The Emotional Sources of 'Chills' Induced by Music." *Music Perception: An Interdisciplinary Journal* 13, no. 2 (1995): 171–207.

Parland, Henry. *Idealrealisation*. Helsinki: Söderströms, 1929.

Projansky, Sarah. *Watching Rape: Film and Television in Postfeminist Culture*. New York: NYU Press, 2001.

Radford, Colin. "Tears and Fiction." *Philosophy* 52 (1997): 208–213.

Rosenberg, Bernard, and David M. White, eds., *Mass Culture: The Popular Arts in America*. Glencoe: The Free Press, 1959.

Ryynänen, Max. "Sending Chills Up My Spine: Somatic Film and the Care of the Self." In *Art, Excess, and Education: Historical and Discursive Contexts*, edited by Kevin Tavin, Mira Kallio-Tavin, and Max Ryynänen, 183–197. New York: Palgrave, 2019.

Ryynänen, Max. *On The Philosophy of Central European Art: The History of an Institution and its Global Competitors*. Lanham: Lexington Books (an Imprint of Rowman and Littlefield), 2020.

Scheller, Jörg. *No Sports! Zur Ästhetik des Bodybuildings*. Stuttgart: Franz Steiner Verlag, 2010.

Seldes, Gilbert. *The 7 Lively Arts*. New York: Harper & Brothers Publishers, 1924.

Seneca, *Moral Letter to Lucilius*, letter 104. C. 65. Wikisource: https://en.wikisource.org/wiki/Moral_letters_to_Lucilius/Letter_104.

Shiner, Larry. *The Invention of Art: A Cultural History*. Chicago and London: The University of Chicago Press, 2001.

Shusterman, Richard. *Pragmatist Aesthetics: Living Beauty, Rethinking Art*. London: Blackwell, 1992.

Shusterman, Richard. *Thinking Through the Body*. Cambridge: Cambridge University Press, 2012.

Sloterdijk, Peter. *The Critique of Cynical Reason*. London: Verso, 1988.

Sobchack, Vivian. *Carnal Thoughts: Embodiment and Moving Image Culture*. Berkeley: University of California Press, 2004.

Tanizaki, Junichiro. *In Praise of Shadows*. Chicago: Leete's Island Books, 1977.

Tatarkiewicz Władysław. *History of Six Ideas*. Warsaw: Polish Scientific Publishers, 1980.

Tavin, Kevin, and Mira Kallio-Tavin. "The Cat, the Cradle, and the Silver Spoon: Violence in Contemporary Art." *Studies in Art Education: A Journal of Issues and Research*, 56, no. 1 (2016): 426–437.

Tervo, Juuso. "Pedagogical Sacrifices: On the Educational Excess of John Duncan's Darkness." In *Art Excess, and Education*, edited by Kevin Tavin, Mira Kallio-Tavin, and Max Ryynänen, 129–144. New York: Palgrave, 2018.

Välimäki, Susanna. *Miten sota soi? Sotaelokuva, ääni ja musiikki*. Tampere: Tampere University Press, 2008.

Walton, Kendall. "Fearing Fictions," *The Journal of Philosophy*, LXXV, no. 1 (January 1978): 5–27.

Williams, Linda. "Film Bodies: Gender, Genre, and Excess." *Film Quarterly* 44, no. 4 (Summer 1991): 2–13.

Yoshioka, Hiroshi. "A Cultural Approach to Sex-related Disgust: Rethinking Shunga and other "perversions" in the 21st Century." In *Cultural Approaches to Disgust and the Visceral*, edited by Max Ryynänen, Heidi Kosonen, and Susanne Ylönen. London – New York: Routledge, Forthcoming 2022.

2 Making It Real: The Need for the Presence of the Body in the Documentation of Contemporary Art

Poet and film maker, Pier Paolo Pasolini wanted to "make it real" just like a rapper. His decadent (bourgeois) ideal was to use "real poor people" to portray the *Lumpenproletariat* in his films, which they nearly always did (in true neorealist fashion). He even went so far as to claim that Italy had lost its (multi)cultural essence (the multi standing for e.g. including an own culture for poor people and the cultures of the regions) through media, modernization and a sort of Westernization (he does not use this word, though), and that he had to travel to Africa and Yemen in order to film more "authentic people" (*Notes Towards an African Orestes*, 1970; *The Walls of Sana'a*, 1971).[1]

In many ways, Pasolini's work accentuated the body as the locus of the real, and one of his most quoted phrases is "I want to express myself by throwing my body into the fight." He fought and had to go to court for that 30 times. Sometimes, there was a philosophical or artistic component, but not always. For example, in a fit of rage he once mugged a gas station employer. The given excerpt, which has become a marginal "hit" in the art field, was originally part of his autobiographical poem *Poet of the Ashes* (*Poeta delle Ceneri*, 1966), written in New York, and it has has inspired many artists and art theorists.[2]

My strongest experiences of the application of the concept happened in Ljubljana, at the Exodos theater festival in 2008, where I saw Raimund Hoghe performing his Maria Callas tribute *36, Avenue Georges Mandel*. In a long talk afterwards, he analyzed his own artistic work (the dancer standing in different poses) through Pasolini's sentence as we, the audience, sat on hard benches (females were offered cushions) in the cold. Hoghe too threw our bodies in a fight, in a sense, but his own was challenged statistically, and also, without doubt, raised questions about the body as he was one of the little people and suffering heavy kyphosis.

DOI: 10.4324/9781003248514-2

Artistically, the body made its most visceral presence in Pasolini's work in the film *Salò, or 120 Days of Sodom* (1975), which portrayed torture through an adaption of Marquis de Sade's novel, brought to Fascist Italy without forgetting the vernacular experiments of *The Trilogy of Life* (1971–1974; *Il Decameron,* 1971; *Canterbury Tales,* 1972; *and Il fiore delle mille e una note,* 1974), where playful, pre-modern and occasionally rustic sexuality played out something really fresh and unseen on the screen, but sadly ended up in the porn sections of video rental shops (this sometimes happened even for *Salò*). However, many of his "fans" remember him for his risky lifestyle, where politics and decadent, bourgeois values often came together in an eccentric way. He provoked both conservative Catholics and the Mafia with his speech and artistic work, for example, by listing the politicians "everyone knew" were corrupted by the criminal organizations (claiming artistic freedom for his "text" to not end up in court again), and he fought with his bare hands members of the terrorist Red Brigades in Venice, during his last visit to that film festival. Many also view his violent death as a logical extension of his artistic and political work. A young prostitute called Giuseppe Pelosi was accused of murdering him. Pasolini was found dead in Ostia (Rome) November 2, 1976. The real murderer has remained a mystery, as it seems that many people could have attacked him, and everyone knew how much he had stirred up hate against himself.

Not many know about Pasolini's late interest in body art, which he explored with Fabio Mauri 5 months before his death.[3] But neither this nor the pathetic, bourgeois attitude Pasolini had when he exalted the less privileged as being more "authentic," nor his assumption of the role of the mythical revolutionary male with a dark side, a type loved by many young middle class men striving to become heroes in their own narrative by exploring the margins from poverty (thus appropriating the culture of the poor) to drugs (this was not Pasolini's thing) and the boundaries of their own sexuality. In this sense, Pasolini is just one man in a long line from Yukio Mishima to Jean Genet, all of them, artistic and interesting and good. (The philosophical icons of the same genre are Maurice Blanchot and Georges Bataille, I suppose.)

But then, the idea of exemplification in the poem is something to examine. Pasolini writes this about exemplification: *Vorrei esprimermi con gli esempi. Gettare il mio corpo nella lotta.* Forgetting the poetic translations, the meaning of this is simply: "I want to express myself with examples. To throw my body into the fight." The poem of which this is just a small fragment, tells the story of Pasolini himself, his lived life; Stefano Casi has called it poetry in action (*poesia in azione*), putting the finger on Pasolini's way of mixing life and art, both working for the same,[4] accentuating the way his life exemplified for his poems what to do, and vice versa. It is about embodying ideas and textualizing embodiment.

To be an example of something, and embodying an idea is something that has a strong role in today's visual art, and in a sense, it is needed for many works of art to be possible. Its role is often presented through documentation. When carrying out their small political acts, executed in the framework of contemporary art, it is virtually never just about fiction. Things have to be *real*, done *for real*, and documented while doing.

One could write a book of manuscripts of political performances, but it would not work in this field. One could say, write

> An African European artist climbs all the way to the top of Agassizhorn (3946 metres), a peak in the Swiss Alpine region, which was named after local 19th century race theorist, Louis Agassiz, and brings her own flag to the top. She gives the peak a new name, Rentyhorn, in homage to a Congolese-born slave called Renty, whom Agassiz ordered to be photographed on a plantation in Carolina "to prove the inferiority of the black race.[5]

The idea reminds me of *Dirty Work,* a performance by Forced Entertainment, (1998, which I saw in 1999 in London), where the performers "alternately compete and work together to imagine and describe a performance as big, as varied, as ugly and as impossible as the whole world" (as the website of the group puts it[6]). Even if the performers talk in a serious manner and provide highly interesting scenes, the effect is banal. *Dirty Work* deals (in a post-Beckett manner) with the relationship of idea and execution; some of the stories are too magnified to be executed, and the role of the manuscript is to actually be the performance itself.

Let's go back to Rentyhorn. When the Haitian-Swiss Sasha Huber does the deed told in the example given earlier, climbing all the way to the top of that peak in the Alps, and documents it, and the presence of her body in the documentation of the act makes it meaningful for the people viewing it. Of course, some will just hammer it pseudo-critically, without listening to the voice of someone who feels over-shadowed and threatened by a dark past which is still visible in landmarks like this, and this is one way to look at it. These critics crave more artistic forms and/or extra layers of intellectual work. For many, however, seeing the woman climb there and perform this act, manifest it and bring it "on stage," feels meaningful. The living artist is what makes this presentation strong, the body that fought the snow, had the stamina, and took the (political) risk, and made the visually thoughtful presentation of it. The body did not just fantasize, like political theorists do (nothing against them, we need them too), and it did not enter into direct political action, but threw over a symbolical threat.

There is another work that exemplifies the presence of the body and how one needs it. Conceptual artist Minna Heikinaho turned her gallery *Push Firma Beige* in Kallio, Helsinki, into a breakfast place for addicts and homeless people, total strangers for her, some of them criminals. For years, in the 1990s, she offered them something to eat. As a story, somewhere, this would function differently than looking at an act that really happened, this woman opening the door for people in the morning, sitting with them, offering food, using the gallery (it truly was a political gallery) for social work, for free (of course). One can just imagine the social stamina needed, the physical presence, and everything, and as the artist herself was not the type that would present this everywhere with touching images, but kept a low profile and really respected the people, it makes a mark on the viewer/listener.

If this were done by a robot, even one controlled by an artist, it would be nothing. Important to note: if it were done by a social worker, it would also be beautiful (for many of us). But, what happens when artists take their body and do things, and produce presentations of it; does their body also become an example of something, exemplifying the political potential we all have, and being about throwing the body into the fight for something?

Of course, it is not the real body we mostly see in this type of cases, but a body in documentation, a documented body doing it. It brings not just "depth" and "weight" to the idea, while embodying it, but it also challenges our bodies when we emphatically look at the images or the possible films, maybe not in the way that we look at moving images and react with our mirror neurons, but in another way, well supported by the image. We put our soul into the real-life protagonist.

Artists intervening with communities to work out a performance with them (bringing real people together, forging them to create more community), supporting people with their legal problems (e.g. filling in forms for administration and the Immigration Service)[7] and, studying, presenting, and analyzing environmental problems, scenes of environmental catastrophes and mediating voices from people who do not have power – these are all forms of work where the difference from activism is in the presentation, and the philosophical, artistic framing that the contemporary art scene supports. I don't claim that this is the most effective way of changing the world (sometimes it might be, of course), but the role of visual documentation is interesting.

Anthropologist Michael Taussig has repeatedly worked with the topic of the weirdly legitimate role of text in reference to images. He has shown how before the arrival of the Europeans other forms of imitation had an interesting epistemological role and functioned as a way of archiving knowledge in many places (like Polynesia), and how Europeans brought with them the idea of the dominance of the text. He has made his fieldbooks, full of his drawings, the core of his work. It is actually weird how we conceive of written descriptions as so important for theoretical thinking, despite the fact that we know how much photographs can tell us too.[8] Photographing fields before and after the effect of new EU laws clearly shows the differences in the landscape,[9] which could also be described textually, but photos alone do not legitimately function as argumentation.

In the very theoretical field of contemporary art, photos and other forms of visual documentation have been precisely about this: the artists want to show something. However, in the case of the aforementioned political art acts, this is not only the case. Thus, the documentation makes political thought concrete, not in the way that the masses in Marx's dreams would have made his theoretical understanding of the workings of history real, but by being represented by images (moving and still) and through the platform of contemporary art, the act becomes very much public. The body becomes public too, and without it the whole act and the publicity that arrives would make no sense; it would all be very shallow.

This has very little to do with beauty or any other aesthetic category, although aestheticians pride themselves on having a special relationship to the arts. The entire project is of a philosophical nature, but not in any sense which Arthur C. Danto's followers with their thoughts about the "artworld" could accentuate as belonging to their "field." For someone working in the manner of Huber or Heikinaho, it is not important if people in key positions in museums and/or the cultural pages of newspapers see their work as "art" because art as a field, a forum, a channel, and a force-field is their instrument. It hosts their body, as a public space, a body that has been documented doing challenging deeds, and presents it in the visual culture of contemporary art. Interestingly, although many people like to think of contemporary art as just a historical follower of visual art, visuality is often no longer in a dominant position in the field. One can celebrate the way that artists show others that they too can do things politically; but although they might want to think that they function as "artivists" who show the possibilities of acti-vism through their partly experimental social acts, sadly, there are not many reasons to think that people would follow their role models. They prefer to follow royals, film stars and, if other artists are to be mentioned, maybe famous writers. Still, this not to say that these deeds would be carried out in vain. For example, Huber has made Agassiz's dark legacy and presence in Switzerland visible for years, and, working together with historian Hans Fässler and the Transatlantic Committee "De-mounting Louis Agassiz," she has affected the rethinking of the issue in her home country. If nothing else, at least the people feeling awkward about this have received a new situation, which is a great result. (Of course, just reaching 300 people in a gallery would be worthwhile too. Why not?) Why should a brown European have to look at a mountain top named like this? Some might say that it is important to preserve history and to save the original name to remember how things were, but mountain tops, statues and memorials do not function neutrally like history writing. They represent societal values, whether one would like to gaze at them neutrally, from a historical point of view or not. The Allied Forces removed the Swastikas when they reached Berlin. Should the Swastikas have been saved for historical reasons?

The presence of the body also removes analytic neutrality from imagined stories. There is a real person. We see her face. We see her body, being there, doing things. Emphatically, as visual perceivers, we engage with her, although we actually see just images. But, these images in the exhibition spaces of contemporary art museums are not just any kind of images that float by. I might see hundreds of media images every day. But, contemporary art has somehow been able to retain the old way of using time with images. The example given, carefully framed, if not aestheticized (this seldom happens today in this type of art), and at least formally well edited, offers a possibility for dialogue with someone, through the presence of the real body in the images portrayed. Concepts and perspectives turn into flesh, although viewed as visual culture in contemporary art.

The motto that you ought to live what you preach is in some sense at stake here too; the visual documentation makes it clear that someone really works on problems by being present somewhere, where things happen, whether symbolically or not. In this sense, contemporary art, when actively documenting this kind of political deed, works like the media coverage of people like Mahatma Gandhi and Nelson Mandela, who have been very important for many people, following the way they embodied their own lives into being part of politics, their bodies up front when photos were taken, lying in prison, fasting, and walking. Huber and Heikinaho do this on a small scale, but still, there is a connection. And, small scales should be praised too. I am not ready to go to prison or be shot for the sake of politics. But, I can do small things, small beautiful acts, and I might think of Huber and Heikinaho when I do them (and when I have done them). In *Somaesthetics: A Disciplinary Proposal,* Richard Shusterman writes the following:

> "Michel Foucault's seminal vision of the body as a docile, malleable site for inscribing social power reveals the crucial role somatics can play for political philosophy." Together with self-styling and dance this is a form of representational somaesthetic practice, where the body is in the center of the action.[10]

The quintessential role that the body plays in different kinds of political orders is something that Foucault really showed us through his idea historical work, *Surveiller et punir* (*Discipline and Punish,* 1975).[11] Foucault's books are central for the art scene, but I am not sure how much artists have thought of their bodies as political instruments in the field of contemporary art. Martin Jay wrote the following about John Dewey's philosophy and its political extensions:

> His vision of democracy necessitated a robust commitment not only to an open-ended process of unimpeded free inquiry, which emulated that of the scientific community, but also to the self-realization that came through active participation in the public sphere. The model of that self-realization he saw best expressed in the sensually mediated, organically consummated, formally molded activity that was aesthetic experience.[12]

Is not this exactly at the core of the practice of political art, where one throws one's body into the fight, in one of the most successful public spheres, where people can be heard? Art is sometimes as "yellow" as the "yellow press" (the tabloids), but still, it is the artist who produces the work and stands for it, not the machinery that is behind media. The term (yellow press) was born of the rivalry between Joseph Pulitzer's *New York World* and William Randolph Hearst's *New York Journal.* They battled for power in N.Y.C. at the turn of the twentieth century, and both papers were accused of being yellow by critics of the populist and sensational press. Erwin Wardman coined the term. He was the editor of the *New York Press* (another competitor). The term was never defined well, but it probably referred to the popular *The Yellow Kid* comic strip at the time. Both Pulitzer and Hearst published it. Although much art can be described as sensationalist and populist, one has the possibility of keeping it real in the sense that I have discussed here; but one can also keep it complex, avoiding simplification, and making it more symbolic than straightforward. Jay's accent on Dewey's work, the way he wants us to remember how much Dewey thought about self-realization through active participation in the public sphere, and art, really, is an area of life where one can achieve this fully, and even reach many people. When critical citizens test the limits of twisted orders, cross tracks institutionally and politically, and perform social patterns in an experimental manner, their example, visible in documentation, but done for real with a real body, and being the body in question, they work to refine the boundary of political imagination and reality. Contemporary artist Dan Graham wrote that "(a)ll artists are alike. They dream of doing something that's more social, more collaborative, and more real than art,"[13] and the fact that the body has become a central instrument in contemporary art is partly about the understanding that this is the way to go "more real than art." Occasionally, this has worked out very well.

Conclusions

Documentation in contemporary art has a somatic role, which we have not understood well enough so far. Presenting the body photographically presents the somatic side of the work to the audience, which can so relate to it. In political art, the documented body works also as an example of our political potentials, as the body of the artist exemplifies what can be done in real life. Sometimes political art makes sense only because there is documentation to look at. Understanding the key role that documentation has might offer a new perspective for interpreting contemporary art. As one new example of the somatic side of images, it reminds us about the strong role of the body in the arts.

Notes

1 On Pasolini's thoughts, see, for example, Pier Paolo Pasolini, *Heretical Empiricism* (Bloomington: Indiana University Press, 1988); Pier Paolo Pasolini, *Il Chaos: L"orrendo universo" del consumo e del potere* (Roma: Editori Riuniti, 1995); and the Pasolini quotes in Franca Faldini and Goffredo Fofi, *L'avventurosa storia del cinema Italiano, raccontata del suoi protagonisti* (Milano: Feltrinelli, 1981). On Pasolini's life and work, see, for

example, Christian Braad-Thomsen, *De uforsonlige* (Copenhagen: Amadeus, 1988) and/or Enzo Siciliano, *Vita di Pasolini* (Milano: Rizzoli, 1978).

2 See, for example, Patrick Steffen in his and Alma Ruiz's interview with Lynda Benglish in *Flash Art International* November-December 2011 ("Lynda Benglish"). Https://flash---art.com/article/lynda-benglis/.

3 Stefano Casi, "Pasolini, il corpo intellettuale," in *Leredità di Pier Paolo Pasolini*, edited by Alessandro Guidi and Pierluigi Sassetti, 39–48. Milano: Mimesis Edizioni, 2009. (Note on page 47.)

4 Casi (2009, 46) sees it as a body where poetry acts, but I am more here stressing the philosophical and political sides of it. "Poetry in action" (poesia in azione) is one expression Casi uses as well to describe Pasolini's way of working (ibid.).

5 See the project presentation on Sasha Huber's webpages: http://www.sashahuber.com/?cat=5.

6 Https://www.forcedentertainment.com/projects/dirty-work/.

7 I am especially thankful to Ange Taggart, Anne Salmela, and Anna Turunen for their work on these issues. It has made me wiser.

8 Michael Taussig, *I Swear I Saw This: Drawings in Fieldwork Notebooks, Namely My Own* (Chicago and London: The University of Chicago Press, 2011).

9 See Tapio Heikkilä, *Visuaalinen maisemanseuranta* (Helsinki: Musta Taide, 2007).

10 Richard Shusterman, "Somaesthetics: A Disciplinary Proposal," *The Journal of Aesthetics and Art Criticism* 57, no. 3 (Summer, 1999): 270.

11 Michel Foucault, *Discipline and Punish* (New York: Pantheon Books, 1977).

12 Martin Jay, "Somaesthetics and Democracy: Dewey and Contemporary Body Art." *Journal of Aesthetic Education* 36, no. 4 (Winter 2002): 55–69.

13 Claire Bishop, *Artificial Hells* (London: Verso: 2012).

Bibliography

Bishop, Claire. *Artificial Hells*. London: Verso, 2012.

Braad-Thomsen, Christian. *De uforsonlige*. Copenhagen: Amadeus, 1988.

Casi, Stefano. "Pasolini, il corpo intellettuale." In *L'eredità di Pier Paolo Pasolini*, edited by Alessandro Guidi and Pierluigi Sassetti, 39–48. Milano: Mimesis Edizioni, 2009.

Faldini, Franca, and Goffredo Fofi. *L'avventurosa storia del cinema Italiano, raccontata del suoi protagonist*. Milano: Feltrinelli, 1981.

Foucault, Michel. *Discipline and Punish*. New York: Pantheon Books, 1977.

Heikkilä, Tapio. *Visuaalinen maisemanseuranta*. Helsinki: Musta Taide, 2007.

Jay, Martin. "Somaesthetics and Democracy: Dewey and Contemporary Body Art." *Journal of Aesthetic Education* 36, no. 4 (Winter 2002): 55–69.

Pasolini, Pier Paolo. *Heretical Empiricism*. Bloomington: Indiana University Press, 1988.

Pasolini, Pier Paolo. *Il Chaos: L'orrendo universo" del consumo e del potere*. Roma: Editori Riuniti, 1995.

Shusterman, Richard. "Somaesthetics: A Disciplinary Proposal," *The Journal of Aesthetics and Art Criticism* 57, no. 3 (Summer 1999): 299–313.

Siciliano, Enzo. *Vita di Pasolini.* Milano: Rizzoli, 1978.

Steffen, Patrick, and Alma Ruiz. "Lynda Benglish." *Flash Art International* November-December 2011. https://flash—art.com/article/lynda-benglis/

Taussig, Michael. *I Swear I Saw This: Drawings in Fieldwork Notebooks, Namely My Own.* Chicago and London: The University of Chicago Press, 2011.

3 Cutting, Mending, Learning

Most of the West has already long dropped the idea of post-modernity and postmodernism, an interesting difference made by the British Isles (and occasionally North America), where the latter concept thrives as a scholarly slur against people who do not apply positivist principles to their academic work, mainly those who are into "continental thinking."[1] The "ism" itself, as an artistic and intellectual movement, looks suddenly also clearly historical – as something that dominated highbrow arts and cultural studies in the 1980s and 1990s. "Postmodernity," referring to an era, has also become a historical concept, which few refer to anymore.

The concept raises memories which show how important it has been to go further. For those of us who were pushing our way from the shadows into the central platforms of theory and thinking from East Europe (*C'est moi*), Asia, Africa and South America, without forgetting the lower classes (*C'est moi aussi*), post-modernism often looked like a social savior of the old power system. In its almost hermetically sealed dialogue with modernism, it still, paradoxically, as it worked hard to decentralize its pre-decessor, kept the game closed for the privileged (mainly middle-class, white[2]) people from dominant Western countries (which mostly had a colonialist history in a way or another) who had been the protagonists of modernism too – here hanging on to still "take care" of major paradigms, although now applying a critical perspective. The turn against the old paradigm was not yet an open MIC for us, if we did not travel to the heart of the West, like London, New York or Paris to work on our careers in the universities there, becoming truly "Western."

When one looks at the much more global field where we all already really meet at least a bit now, even if some countries keep on dom-inating more than necessary, the difference is huge. Asian, African

DOI: 10.4324/9781003248514-3

and South American contemporary artists made their way to the top of the art world in the early 2000s. Films and TV series from all over the world reach us better, not just through technological development, but through becoming at least a bit more "just films" and "TV series" like any TV series – on Netflix, for example. It was hard to predict what a more global culture could become – and we still do not really have a name for the position in which we find ourselves now. Anglo-American culture might still dominate, maybe even more than ever, but still, everywhere I go, there is at least some access to a more global world and its platforms, networks and connections, and people who have made it to a platform, even if they are not from a major Western scene.

Some of the works and artists that were thought of as a being "postmodern" or "postmodernist" at the peak of the movement might also no longer necessarily look like it, if one does not focus on historical readings stressing the era. Maybe some novels by Umberto Eco, Don DeLillo or Bret Easton Ellis embody a feeling of "representing" postmodernism (literature might be the field where the era/ism left its clearest permanent traces, together with architecture) – but mostly the movement that stressed and prophesized the end of "objective" knowledge as much the end of high and low (and grand narratives) and stressed irony, self-referentiality and relativism, feels now like an interpretative marinade that has dripped off many of the works that were claimed to embody its very nature.

I recall Quentin Tarantino's films and Paul McCarthy's contemporary art being called postmodernist, but now the way Tarantino's films were thought of as somehow dominantly performatively intertextual "games" looks like a very technical interpretation of them. McCarthy's disgust-driven works of art show another side of the story. The use of popular culture idioms, amusement park tech (clumsy machines showing violent scenes) and (this probably felt like something when McCarthy started) easygoing colors for sure made sense in the interpretative territory built and offered by the postmodernists, where all this was about demolishing the gray and anal impact of modernism.

There is more to it, though. The body is there, through the disgust and uncanny hair-raising provoked by, for example, films like McCarthy's *Painter* (1995), where a grotesque, uncanny figure works with an enormous brush, and (collaboration with Mike Kelley) *Heidi* (1992), where masks, sausages (excreted by a "body-double" puppet) and goo dominate. Now this side, disgust and other somatic reactions, looks more like what the works were about, and for sure, this might have been the case also in the original context in many ways, but the interpretative model that was offered in the 1990s often still kept overshadowing the body and our reactions to the seen.

Although there was body art[3] and the philosophical work of Jean-Luc Nancy and Luce Irigaray put the spotlight on the *corpus*[4] – one cannot here forget either the way gym training, food diets and other body cultures started to grow, too, at the time[5] – somehow the body gained attention in philosophy and cultural studies dominantly through ideas of the body as machine. Cybernetics and fantasies of body hacking and robotics[6] were maybe in some sense part of the texture of the works of art, too, but not to an extent that should have overshadowed the way our organic body was often the main target of many films and works of art.

This is maybe most evident if one thinks of David Cronenberg's films. When one thinks of films like *Videodrome* (1983), and when one looks at it now, it is less the tech side of it that raises eyebrows, but what it shows about our sense of the body and what it does to our bodies (when we view the film), from somatic reflection to reactions like disgust. And we live through the bodily functions on screen with our own ones, like echoing body-doubles.

Of course, the concept of body horror (organic horror and biological horror mainly just mash-up with this concept, but there are differences, too) that Linda Williams came up with in 1991 in her analysis of bodily excess in film,[7] in her analysis of certain types of films that Carol J. Clover had called "body genres,"[8] was on the rise in film studies. In this era, this is something that became increasingly commonplace in mainstream culture, or at least very close to what could be called mainstream. From pornographic production to slasher, horror and just otherwise, very physical movies became a commonplace.

Could it be that excess, somatic film, awkwardness and disgust – together with other reactions that dominate the "scene" (eroticism, awe) – could together actually become something that we remember from our era as something that in the future pinpoints its difference than other eras? Or did we just turn a new page in human culture for a longer "friendship" with disgustification, somatification and horrorification?

One could argue that these cultural features do not dominate all lives, nor do they dominate even the whole lives of the people who mainly consume them. But this is always the case. This is how, for example, the Romantic era worked, too, of course. Not everyone was "romantic."

Taking us back to the excess of the 1980s and 1990s, which still looks very much aestheticized in contrast to the reality-driven presentation of giant spiders on faces and/or people eating slime on primetime which we testify today, there is an interesting connection, though, to what happened during the romantic time. We are already accustomed to thinking that (artistic and sentimental, not the simplest everyday) kitsch would partly take forward the legacy of romanticism,[9] and we know how the Gothic revival had a key role in romanticism and how it still dominates some strands of popular culture today from architecture to horror films, but the way the romantic era, together with other threads of somatic history, poses questions and hints for us on our own condition and for our future could offer an interesting philosophical path to wander. My discourse on it will not suffice to say something grand about romanticism itself, nor about other historical periods (not even about today's contemporaneity), but I hope to build on interesting connections that we might want to lay our hands on a bit more, in our quest to understand what kind of conditioned animals we are today.

Chopin's Heart

Visiting the University of Warsaw, a couple of years ago, my friend and colleague (who had kindly invited me to give a talk) Adam Andrzejewski said, just as a side comment as we went for something to eat after my talk, that I should visit the Holy Cross Church close to the campus – as Chopin's heart is there.

I went in, of course, and there it was. On one of the central pillars there was a sign of the type "here lived" with the text: "Here rests the heart of Frederic Chopin." Chopin had died in France in 1849, but he expressed a morbid wish, which might sound bizarre and even ridiculous – but which was actually not that exceptional (though still rare) at the time. He asked to have his heart removed after his death and then taken back to his homeland, i.e. Poland (the rest of his body was buried at Pere Lachaise).[10]

As we know that Chopin was a romantic composer and he lived and worked during the romantic era, the story gains a certain sense of inner logic, which does not leave the case to the individual Chopin alone, but to the artistic and cultural context, too. Chopin, though, was afraid that he would become paralyzed and then accidentally be buried alive. That is why he insisted that his close ones would confirm with a doctor, who would perform an autopsy on his body, that he was dead. But, then, burying hearts separately from the rest of the body had been sometimes and in some regions of Europe a practice which existed already in the Middle Ages in the form Chopin had it done – for the European aristocracy. Sometimes during crusades someone died in a heathen place. Bringing the whole body back was at the time virtually impossible, but one could bring the heart back, for example, and following the heart's symbolic role, it made sense to bury the heart back home.[11] Skeletons with inner organs were brought home and buried.

Members of the French and English aristocracy made this uncanny practice into a bit more of an everyday practice in the late Middle Ages, and then heart burial gained some sort of symbolic role in European upper-class culture in the seventeenth century. Kings, queens, and popes (Richard the Lion-Heart, Leo XIII) asked that their hearts be buried in some spot they had liked. The prince-bishops of Würzburg even made this into a family practice of generations.[12] The Bavarian tradition called for the extraction of the heart, when Kings were buried, so that the (in)famous, decadent Ludwig II, a friend of Richard Wagner and the commissioner of Neuschwanstein Castle (the romantic model for Disney's Sleeping Beauty Castle and a symbol for the whole romantic era) is buried in München although his heart is in Altötting's Chapel of Grace.[13] Then, eventually, romantic poets took up the idea, for obvious, "aesthetic" reasons, one could say: Percy Shelley's wife Mary, who was not shy in fantasizing about reconstructions of "human beings" in her *Frankenstein* (1818), brought his heart to England, as the poet died in the Bay of Lerici on the Italian coast in 1822. As the heart itself is, if anything in the human body, really machine-like, the story connects in an uncanny way to the novel.

Chopin, as a romantic subject, added to his wish, "take my heart back to my *native land,*" in the nationalist spirit of the era, in a way which today makes one only think of populist right-wing politics, but which at the time had a profound connection to the cultural turn (fueled by German romantic philosophy) that had made people think of their languages and geographical positions.

We can just imagine what some people with a lot of imagination who hung out with Percy Shelley or the prince-bishops of Würzburg would have done if they had had our technology to play with. Some of that fantasy can of course be found in Mary Shelley's book *Frankenstein.*

Still, Chopin's story connects also in some sense artistically to the way some contemporary artists have made the body into a playground, in a way, so that if someone asked for a favor of Chopin's type, it would sound understandable in some artistic contexts today. The connection might sound banal, but it is worth taking a look at.

Art where the body is mutilated, in one way or another, deliberately by the artist, is maybe not a "genre," but it is a "thing" today. We have plenty of examples to look at. ORLAN, originally a performance artist, became a pioneer in carnal art and "nomadic somaesthetics" (as one could nail it) through her experiments with body surgery in the 1990s (e.g. 1993 implants on the forehead). She became most famous through her project of reincarnating herself in an iconographical way into visually becoming (through sculpting her own body) women of famous paintings and sculptures of art history.

Another mark of the time and its possibilities, an artist with a tech experimentalist and radically somaesthetic attitude, is Stelarc, who claims that the human body is obsolete, and who has worked, for example, through piercing, growing a human ear in his arm (grown from his own flesh), and radical flesh hook suspension.[14] By no means am I claiming that ORLAN or Stelarc are the most excessive pioneers of body mutation, but the way they do/did it, the context where they made/make it is meaningful, an artistic context with wide distribution and a readymade body-driven audience. Nobody would really be surprised if Stelarc or ORLAN suddenly asked to have one body part removed after their death, and, for example, implant it into a robot or another artist (they could even exchange ears or eyes when dead: no one would really be surprised to hear if this was the case). And the same applies, in some sense, to artists like Moon Ribas, who implanted a sensor which helps her to feel earthquakes all over the world, and Neil Harbisson, who has an antenna implanted in his skull.

Of course, to a smaller extent, working on the body is an issue everywhere from tabloids and women's magazines to diets and feel-good lessons, as already noted earlier in this book. Mainly they are far from extreme, or at least the intention is not to produce or provoke excess – although that easily happens too, of course, when people become too monomanic with their practices. People apply Paleolithic diets (which actually is the diet most Europeans had before the Romans took over half of the continent and started growing wheat[15]), or macrobiotics, and go too far in their hunt for an authentic lifestyle, putting themselves and/or their children in danger. And it is not just any authenticity, but a holistic, harmonic one that most people seem to seek: lifestyles with a feeling of organicity dominate, mindfulness and processes where people's fragmented whole is somewhat mended into being one balanced whole. Whatever the grounds and the grounding experiences (many of us feel fragmentation which they claim comes from today's world and culture), these lifestyles can of course bring out a difference, and make life more pleasant. No doubt about it.

Art has aimed for quite the opposite – at least when it has made the spotlight, like in the cases recalled above.[16] This is, of course, at least partly because of the fact that contemporary art's methods bring forth the heritage of countering, shocking and questioning, which the modernists and avant-gardists of the twentieth century, in different ways, applied in their quest to make a difference, that we do not easily even think of moderate, softly impact-driven acts fueled by everyday aspirations as easily as "art" – although the suprematists, for example, with Kazimir Malevich, the icon of modernism, at the front, aimed for that in their early twentieth-century program. When the body has been turned into a stage of experimental practices, into a post-sculpture, or an object of artistic expression, it has not just tempted the tabloids and the sensational media to catch up with it. It has been easy to write art history from the point of view that something is being taken beyond our expectations and horizon when an artist like Alejandro Jodorowsky and other members of the Panic Movement in Paris in the 1960s crucified a chicken and covered a naked woman in honey (Sacramental Melodrama, 1965), than when someone is applying art to healing practices, which in art circles sounds immediately like commercial or new age culture and "nothing new." It is not that we wouldn't have recognized the other side of bodily driven art too. There are plenty of exhibitions on, for example, healing practices in art.[17] But the body there seems to be less "radical" for many, and we might want to challenge that notion. I recall a lecture by Richard Shusterman in 1998 (in Helsinki), where he said that people focus on Foucaldian exercises like S/M sex in their quest to cross boundaries, at the same as their own most excessive experience might be that they finally, after decades, reached out and hugged their father.

We gain a lot of information, though, from excessive works of art – and they push us to reflect. Thinking about the tech and body operations side of art, although the first reaction to ORLAN, Stelarc, Ribas and Harbisson might be an experience of the uncanny, we easily also reflect on ourselves, for example the way our teeth are actually partly plastic, our glasses and medications for depression (supporting the machinery to change to the light side), our pacemakers and prosthesis are not organic, "authentic" nor original, but make us into living mass culture. Works of art of the type described above push us to reflect on ourselves and the technological development that surrounds us and already pierces our bodies.

We might not be so much cyborgs, as we used to fantasize in the 1990s, but on the other hand, in the everyday, we still too often feel and experience ourselves to be organic or natural. Experiencing and identifying ourselves to be things could slowly be on the rise, though, and it might be the time to start bringing us on par with our situation philosophically, as well.

Not that this would not have happened already to some extent. Looking at Gilles Deleuze's and Felix Guattari's work from this point of view, the turn to start viewing ourselves not just as animals but also, to some extent, *just* machines, simply, profanely, without any sci-fi imagination in *Capitalism and Schizophrenia* (1972, 1980), and noticing that the body works quite like a machine or even a factory in many respects, is still not something that we would have integrated to our everyday thinking.

"It is at work everywhere, functioning smoothly at times, at other times in fits and starts. It breathes, it heats, it eats. It shits and fucks. [...] Everywhere it is machines – real ones, not figurative ones: machines driving other machines, machines being driven by other machines, with all the necessary couplings and connections. An organ-machine is plugged into an energy-source-machine: the one produces a flow that the other interrupts. The breast is a machine that produces milk, and the mouth machine coupled to it. The mouth of the anorexic wavers between several functions: its possessor is uncertain as to whether it is an eating-machine, an anal machine, a talking-machine, or a breathing machine (asthma attacks). Hence we are all handymen: each with his little machines,"[18] Deleuze and Guattari write. It is of course not that this experience should stay with us throughout our everyday, but thinking about all the automatizations of our body from the communication of the cells to the way the body (often by itself, if we just sit down), for example, "shits" (as they write), and the way it works (for us), it would be more than natural that we would also see this side of the body from time to time as our companion in the everyday. Thinking about the way human-created chemicals (through medication and food), limbs and other apparatus from glasses to plastic teeth are part of our formation as much as reading, gazing at images and discussing, it just feels like a big lie to dream about humanity the way it is still done, stressing "totally" organic individuals with holistic experiences. Not that this lie should make us worried, nor that there is anything to "reveal" – but would not increasingly many be interested in not just thinking of us as just (at least a bit) things, too?

In 1994 Mario Perniola wrote *Il sex appeal dell'inorganico* (*The Sex Appeal of the Inorganic*, 2004), where our thingness found its way into the spotlight for the first time.[19] One dead end for humanist body metaphysics, the book discussed our way of being things, in-organic, and the way we, from time to time, already start experiencing it more openly, realizing it, understanding it, coping with it. One could say that Perniola had a great deal of enthusiasm about thingness.

Whatever our ideologies, values and/or identities say, and whether or not our everyday discourse matches it, there are moments when we experience our thingness, our being like commodities or machines. Perniola approaches it with a broader, systematic analysis of colder, commodified and/or non-holistic sides of experience. While most aestheticians have kept on cherishing, for example, holistic, harmonic experience – in the footsteps of Dewey, this has become a *pathos* in pragmatism – or experiences where balanced disinterested judgment prevails (the Kantian tradition), Perniola discusses the narrow experiences of the "cool" and "high" in contemporary culture in *Contro comunicazione* (2004).[20] He is not digging himself in to the long history of the "cool" that has its origins on the Ivory Coast, and which, with richness and heritage, flourishes on a John Coltrane record, but on the contemporary cultural loose and narrow, non-emotional and "whatever"-natured cool that fills the talk of, for example, an everyday middle-class white American, with an impact then on the whole globe. The high (not the brow, but the high gained, for example, from drug abuse), on the other hand, is also stripped of all emotions and holism. It is a drive, physical and mental elevation, not sublimation, but just a rise in energy levels, and a simple, stingy experience of pleasure. By accentuating new somatic sides of experience that match the afore-mentioned margins of humanity, where there is no holistic human being in the spotlight, Perniola builds a broader idea of a less holistic network of culture and experiences that we live in.

Perniola uses the concept of the inorganic. One of its meanings is simply unnatural, but more broadly speaking, when we encounter the concept in everyday culture, we often talk about inorganic materials. While organic ones are based on plants or animals, the non-organic are not.

Classically one would think that the inorganic lacks authenticity. But the inorganic challenges us with another alternative line of metaphysics. Perniola digs up a thread about the magic of the objects and commodities and the everyday experience of being just a thing, expanding on our self-understanding. When one thinks of it, it is not that rare for us to feel like being treated just like things, or for us to experience ourselves to be "just things," objects or commodities, in one way or another.

Often the experiences we have are, of course, somewhat negative in this regard. And our discourse is often critical about this issue for a reason. Laura Mulvey's point on the "male gaze" (in the already classical article "Visual Pleasure and Narrative Cinema," 1975) is a good example of a philosophical reaction toward a way to turn women into objects in visual culture, in the text, namely film.[21] Men become objectified visually far less, and it is less a structural issue in the society and its power-relations, but of course, in a world increasingly dominated by visual culture such as social media and reality TV, it is no wonder that this would grow into an unpleasant collective experience, too. Mulvey's heterosexual, masculine gaze – today one could maybe say that it represents certain forms of aggressive masculinities – works through film to use female bodies to provide pleasure for the men gazing at the females subjected to them.

I am convinced that far more people in my community do experience this, although they do not discuss it, for moral reasons and for the reason that it is untrendy, but another way to look at it would be that one realizes the differences between the biological (somatic) gaze and the cultural gaze here. We do not always choose the things that provide us with pleasure, nor is everything culturally or politically laden. Television and all visual media, more or less, depend on the amount of visual orientation and sensitivity in the viewer, biological, too, although it is often hard to point out where the *bios* ends and culture starts. Sometimes the body leads, and we might not like it – and this applies to both males and females[22]. Sometimes, on the other hand, culture leads. And this also applies to how we present ourselves. For whatever social and cultural reasons, some people like to be objects of other people's gazes and actions, more than others, and this differs very much with the culture. Some even like to be "male-gazed" (or "female-gazed," see footnote 101), and it is tricky to just criticize that. Some might not realize their destiny in a sexist system, but some do, and still like it, even consciously. The variety of ways to position oneself and find pleasure in social roles and hierarchies are endless – and so are our pleasures of thingness and experiencing oneself to be a bit like a machine, too. One need only to take a look at S/M to get the point of the possibilities in the extremes, but in a more moderate way, we all in differing everyday positions have differing mash-ups of traditions, conventions, power-relations and roles in this respect.

Some of us search for second skins by using PVC clothes. Many males are content if they are called "machines" in bed. Some desire to lose themselves and their feeling of being individual bodies, being just a part of a strobe-lighted mass moving like robots in techno. There are moments when we realize that our partners for a moment just forget us, and use us, like tools – and this does not always feel bad. The same applies to us sometimes being part of teams in sport and/or at work, where subjectivity and individuality are somehow at least experientially lost for the sake of becoming one with a collective machine. And although many say that they want doctors to work more holistically with our bodies, some comfort (and maybe even a sort of psychological safety) might sometimes also lie in the way some doctors treat us like broken machines or things. All this happens to people who are capable of individuation and holistic thinking about themselves. And the experience, itself, of becoming or being just a thing has become more central for us lately, for sure, and that might have to do as much with the increasingly complex nature of things and machines today, and the amount of them that surround us.

One of the ways Karl Marx worked on objects and their role in life (and capitalism) was his idea of the "fetishism of the commodity." He attempted to describe how objects sometimes gathered more value than one would expect, thinking about the work needed for preparing them and the interpersonal relations behind their production. This grew into a description of the network of things themselves, their relative and connected systems of value, which is one of the foundations of Marx's work. Marx compared this form of capitalist cultural estrangement, the cultural "life" of products, to religion.[23] But he also decentralized human beings to some extent, to be objects.

In the so-called "Wood Theft Debates" (1842) of early philosophical Marx, he, as Erica Sherover underlines, while defending the right of the poor to collect branches (in the Rhineland Province), did not just neatly talk about this type of practice as "the customary right of poor in all countries"[24] (and not a local issue), but also equated the (in Hegel's words "incorporated") poor with "objects which can never acquire the character of private property."[25] The ontological correspondence that Marx built between fallen wood and the position of the poor in civil society is not all, as he even claims that "[h]uman poverty senses this kinship."[26] This idea led Marx (idealistically, and romantically) to underline that the poor are the only ones who have not been deceived by the capitalist system. They don't confuse the human with the non-human, "an alien material being."[27] Further, the poor are not victims of fetishistic thinking. Sherover writes: "He [Marx] notes that the so-called 'savages of Cuba regarded gold as a fetish of the Spaniards' and he claims that if these so-called 'savages' had been sitting in the Rhine Provincial Assembly they would have 'regarded wood as the Rhinelanders' fetish'."[28] They would have seen through the mystification, as the poor understood that wood is only wood, not endowing it with a soul.[29]

While Marx saw revolutionary potentials in the (fantasized, maybe even exoticized) purity of the poor (that he embodied through his work[30]), but did not dive into the structure of the allure itself, Walter Benjamin, in his footsteps, with a jab toward Marx, had a take on it.

"If the soul of the commodity which Marx occasionally mentions in jest existed, it would be the most pathetic ever counted in the realm of souls, for it would have to see in everyone the buyer in whose hand and house it wants to nestle. Empathy is the nature of the intoxication to which the flâneur abandons himself in the crowd. 'The poet enjoys the incomparable privilege of being himself and someone else as he sees fit. Like a roving soul in search of a body, he enters another person whenever he wishes. For him alone, all is open; if certain places seem closed to him, it is because in his view they are not worth inspecting' ('Les Foules'). The commodity itself is the speaker here. Yes, the last words give a rather accurate idea of what the commodity whispers to a poor wretch who passes a shop-window containing beautiful and expensive things. These objects are not interested in this person; they do not empathize with him. In the sentences of the significant prose poem 'Les Foules' there speaks, with other words, the fetish itself which Baudelaire's sensitive nature resonated so powerfully; that empathy with inorganic things which was one of his sources of inspiration,"[31] Benjamin writes. "I am an old boudoir full of faded roses": Benjamin continues and so takes up his old romance with poetry and quotes Charles Baudelaire – and he, also someone who likes to find resonating equations between people and things, goes on to talk about machines. He claims that the fast-paced mechanically driven working conditions that dominate the lives of the workers (and which most of us "know by heart" from Charles Chaplin's somatically stimulating movie *Modern Times*, 1936), the way we are in our quotidian life and its (as well) fast-paced traffic surrounded by a machinery of codes and (traffic) signs which challenge our perception and experiential system and the *Shock* driven nature of amusement park entertainment (without forgetting, of course, the better-recalled effects of film montage) are not just challenging our perception and experience, but also partly (especially in the case of the amusement parks) answer our new experiential needs (like film does, too).[32] Chaplin's film, published the same year as the Artwork essay, turns the worker into a machine – not coincidentally.

While sci-fi authors fantasize about a big leap in our relationship to machines, they (and we easily) also tend to forget how we have merged and become one with machines already now – so that part of the fantasy about the future and the way robots will blur our sense of humanity is probably just partly a reflection of our lives today, which somehow slips our attention and consciousness. (Increasingly intelligent) Cars, digital equipment, electronic doors, razors, mobiles, electric bikes and lawnmowers have slowly invaded us, become our extensions, partners "species"[33] and things that in Marx's sense at least somehow might be seen to have a soul. The start of their strong invasion in the 1930s cannot just be seen in Benjamin's work. It shines in John Dewey's sudden existentialist, holistic approach to culture, creativity and nature in *Art as Experience* (1934), which was written at the heyday of Chicago's industrial wealth – and in Martin Heidegger's thinking, that at the same year as Benjamin's "Artwork" essay was finished (1936), wrote in his *Origin of the Work of Art* (1935–1936), and later in his *Discourse on Thinking* (1957) how works of art were often wrongly conceived of as objects, how our lives were dominated by machines like airplanes, and how the production system in the Rühr sucked in people who lost their ("real") roots.[34]

Today's shocks and problems, at least in the West, are less conceived to be machine-related and geographical. Shock might be even more central to us than it ever was in Benjamin's time, but we do not much reflect upon it – as it is commonplace. Whether urban or rural, we are almost daily shocked by horror films, war footage and floods on the news – without forgetting the way clickbait Internet journalism shows us operations gone wrong, professional athletes breaking a bone or oversized spiders found in Australian homes. And all this happens more somatically than Benjamin realized, although he hints at the somatic side of it throughout his writings.

Once in the West we were thought to be atomized into our homes, family by family (gazing at the TV) – but now we are even more atomized, as we gaze by ourselves on our laptops and smart phones. Children sit in groups, all watching their own phones. But more importantly, there is a new cultural paradigm that we are all in, somehow. It concerns the way somatic stimulation has increasingly taken over mass culture and the media. Historically, intellectuals have criticized the masses for passive consuming. But all the time the "masses" have read intellectually simple-minded romances with active hearts and bodies. They have exercised their stomachs with the help of thrillers and horror movies. And they have jumped from their chairs when a hand has popped up from the grave in the end of *Carrie* (1976), felt new sensations in their bodies in amusement parks and found their sexualities (and the ways their organs work) through watching intellectually boring pornographic movies. A short historical ride into the philosophy of passivity, activity and pedagogy might offer some insights into this, I hope. At least it is worth a try.

Passive, Active, and Passive-Active: Notions on Aesthetic Democracy

Jacques Rancière is one of the great storytellers of philosophy – although one could say that he often works hard to find someone else to tell their story. In *Proletarian Nights: The Workers' Dream in Nineteenth-Century France* (1981)[35] it was the nineteenth-century urban poor, whose letters show their (to many) surprising level of societal understanding. Karl Marx, a hyper-active author of various texts, a journalist and writer, had really, according to Rancière, over-emphasized his own role in producing new thought. Rancière shows, through the letters that workers sent to each other, that they understood society well, and often in surprising accordance with Marx. While a typical way of thinking for Marxists is that the poor gain the consciousness and understanding needed for the revolution through their life-situation, in the end someone needs to come from the university to explain it all to them. This was all wrong, according to Rancière.

In *The Ignorant Schoolmaster* (*Le maître ignorant*, 1987), the story – which in the earlier book was a cluster of stories that showed the way – is led by a historical figure, an early nineteenth-century teacher called Joseph Jacotot. He taught at the University of Louvain. Today our pedagogy is full of activating exercises – when I just lecture, some students even thank me for not "activating them" with any exercises as they are so fed up with that kind of pedagogy – but at the time, this way of thinking had not yet taken over. Jacotot's groundbreaking idea was that one could help others learn things that one had not mastered oneself. He explored this himself, through exercises with which he trained students of Flemish (he did not speak Flemish). The idea was to lead the youth to become teachers of themselves. The social implications of the results – their grades were not much different from the grades that classical addresser-addressee and/or "banking method" teachers (at the time they might have been more rigid then today) were able to produce – led him to think, very naturally, about the revolutionary potentials of his new-found practice.

Jacotot became the wandering teacher of self-teaching – in the "shady neighborhoods." He knocked on doors and visited houses that could not afford education, and hoped to teach the parents how they could help their children to teach themselves. The story, explained in detail in Rancière's book, is one of the main foundations of what Rancière called intellectual democracy. It hit like a torpedo the values of the bourgeois at the time. Jacotot did not change society (although he left a grand mark on pedagogy, at least through Rancière's work). He just produced a scandal – and he was fired.[36] Thinking about the active-passive dichotomy, this shows a totally opposite way of thinking than what Marx had – and a more idealistic assumption of what children and students knew and could do by themselves.

This track was not new for Rancière. In *The Philosopher and His Poor*, he had already gone through a whole thread of scholarly attitudes toward the "weak" and the "poor," starting from antiquity and Plato's critical views on craft and climbing all the way up to nineteenth-century socialists, whose fantasies about the poor and their revolutionary potentials were a key element in, for example, Marx's work. Rancière shows in his work how the lower stratum of society has long been interpreted to be somewhat intellectually passive and not conscious of its societal role and the society it lives in, and although Marx gave it a key role in his predictions of societal change, even there, to some extent, they kind of needed a philosopher to step down from his podium and explain things.

Marx, who was possessed by Hegel's dialectics, stressed, besides the shared obsession with consciousness, the idea of clash. Hegel's dialectical system, i.e. thesis, anti-thesis, and synthesis – the modes of historical development – was written to explain how a dynamic phenomenon (that already hides the seed of its own negation) produces a counter phenomenon, and how this is elevated (*Aufhebung*) into a higher state of things. In Marx's reading this (in)famously grew into a societal interpretation of a negative state of things, capitalism, which through its own ethical and even practical impossibility grew its own anti-thesis, i.e. the critique and the reaction against this – which was to be dissolved in a higher form of society.

Already in the Frankfurt School, most notably in Theodor Adorno's writings, the clash itself, the antagonism, anti-thesis i.e., becomes the main thing. The masses no longer, according to the critical Frankfurters, have the potentials needed for revolution, and they turn, in this vision, passive, in some sense. According to Adorno's (and Max Horkheimer's) interpretation of the (Western) society (they lived in, in Germany and then in the US), the masses were unable to change anything – and they did not even possess a consciousness that would make this possible. The reason for this was found in the fact that they noticed that nothing like Marx's idea of revolution had really happened – and they did not doubt Marx's basic idea of the dialectics that would lead to this, but just concluded that society itself has to have changed. The reason was found in art and culture, a component that neither Marx himself, nor Engels, much cared about in the nineteenth century – maybe at least partly because the production of culture was not yet very developed. Synthesis had, according to Adorno, become impossible, although society was still unbearably unequal and oppressive, as the "culture industry," not just mass culture but also the whole hedonistic and consumerist way of dealing with art and everyday culture, worked like a glue to keep the schizophrenic whole together (according to Adorno and Horkheimer). The state of its own impossibility, its dominance and the reactions against it (anti-thesis) did not lead to any kind of development, as people were falsely happy consuming (neatly packaged concert series of "classical music" and) popular music and film, and so the whole society was in a constant state of negative dialectics. Interestingly, Adorno also robbed the "evil capitalists" of their role, and suddenly, for the first time in Marxist thinking, nobody, in this theory, was any longer consciously pulling the strings, but non-subjective forces, a kind of a master's voice, kept things turning like they did – also the "rulers" just enjoying their consumption, partly, it seems, unconsciously.[37]

This attitude turned into images only in the work of the situationists, most notably Guy Debord's pioneering open source book *Society of the Spectacle* (1967), where everything that was left to connect people in what we call a society is the bombardment of images that they live in. Sharing the view with the Christian conservatives that the uneducated Westerner is part of a passive flock that is manipulated with mass culture, Debord and his comrades roused an absurdist micro-movement against this system with their publications, performances and acts.[38] Marx had still been dreaming of firing the bombastic potentials of the less privileged, but together with the growing middle class, they had become a passivated, happy and relatively well-fed horde in these critical theories that rose to prominence after the Second World War.

Historically, our idea of education, still present in the addresser-adressee formula of teaching which still dominates even universities, making the "masses" into something that has to be activated – and in relationship to culture this is often the case, too. Even if many would defend mass culture, they would often conclude that sometimes you don't just need to be active. Theater has somehow quite dominantly merged these two approaches – which is something that Rancière notes in *The Emancipated Spectator*.[39] There, the wrestling with the "passive viewer" has been the strongest in all the arts. Brecht, in the footsteps of the Russian formalists and their theories, and the clearly alienating Chinese theater performances that he had seen, went for alienation, and Artaud fought to pull the viewers from their comfort zone into becoming one organic community for at least the duration of the performance – but both dealt with the people like bio-*materia* they had to animate. And this is still quite typical of theater performances, where we often, when entering, ask ourselves if we will again be engaged and activated (hopefully not, we say), as we have so many times been provoked, maybe even picked up on, or intentionally shocked.

Let's turn our gaze upon the "passive viewer." Mostly they are defined on the base of the use of intellect – and culturally the opponent of the activator is film or television. Both Brecht and Artaud desired to force viewers to be something else than a basic film audience – and virtual reality theorist Jaron Lanier propagated in the 1990s that VR will kill television.[40] Noël Carroll, in his work defining "mass art," writes that one should not underestimate aesthetically Spike Lee films, for example. They "activate the audience to think about problems in society."[41]

How on earth did the accent land so heavily upon discursive and conceptually intellectual practices? Marx himself, as Samir Gandesha and Jonathan Hartle stress, had a sort of an aesthetic idea of the sensual understanding of work that the workers possess,[42] and Adorno's idealization of works of art (the minority of them that he approved of), like Kazimir Malevich's square paintings, Arnold Schönberg's atonal music and Samuel Beckett's absurdist theater, which, in a totally negativized society did not compromise for the *hedone*, but crystallized the very nature of reality, was based on a view that the works, not discursively but technically, taken to their aesthetic conclusion, showed truth, and did so mainly in an obscure, sensual way. But where is our understanding of the sensual in mass culture, the body? It is not that mass culture would create riddles, but its very physical nature, where nothing else is actually promised – this is what Adorno appreciates in circus although he is against most other forms of entertainment in the 1940s[43] – activates the soma more than what ever happens in highbrow culture.

We watch movies and/or TV series at home. Although we lie on the couch, and look like we're just on the receiving end, possibly even with our brains "shut off," reactions to the seen and heard run through the body. We gain chills in the spine, tensions in the neck, tenseness in the stomach – and relief, itching of the soles, skin orgasms, and we laugh, and our chest warms up.

In the end, to take the idea of the passive viewer to its logical end, seen from an intellectual point of view, maybe we are objects for the massage of the film, who sometimes turn even into ragdolls when the going gets tough. When we are tired, this might look even more evident, as we might enter a deep mental state, close to dreaming. As extensions of what we see, our eyes being the plugs through which the filmic reality leaks in, is still a state where the body is more broadly active than when we work with laptops or walk to the shop. It would be saying too much to name it "thinking through the body," as the body here thinks without much reflection, being the total opposite of the situation that most modern and contemporary artists want from their audiences. Like Franz Brentano gave philosophy of mind a new life when he discussed thinking also as something that did not always require a conscious attitude[44] we might have to rethink the body to be active also when someone is just lying on the couch and not actively doing anything.

The aforementioned description connects to thingness. The touch of the film might be cold. There are film directors who have consciously worked on the impersonal touch. For example, some of David Cronenberg's films, like *Videodrome* (1983), leave us cold and alone in our bodies, surrounded by an uncanny atmosphere. Also the use of masks, as in John Carpenter's *Halloween* (1978) or Stanley Kubrick's *Eyes Wide Shut* (1999), do not always just accentuate the cold state of the person portrayed in the film, but can extend the feeling to the viewer themselves. It would be easy to just note that the authors of these filmic products are witty and skillful enough to find the threshold for what makes us feel disturbed, but as art has always also helped us cope with issues – Carol Talon-Hugon asks if one of the reasons for us having art might have been our need to find ways to cope with disgusting phenomena[45] – more questions could be asked about this practice. Do these films, for a reason, also support our need to cope with an increasing experience of us just being a bit like things, or, more plainly, things? The modern reflection on the analogy of us and machines has long been an increasing topic and theme in artistic work. If a broken gramophone was just a metaphor for the broken psyche of the protagonist in Henry Parland's novel *To Pieces* (*Sönder*) (1932),[46] man became machine-like in Charlie Chaplin's *Modern Times* (1936), and today, machines have aspirations and strategic thinking – already the computer of the space ship in Stanley Kubrick's *Space Odyssey 2001* (1968) took over to take lead of its own destiny – and they both learn from human beings and teach us, a theme that gained wide acceptance and popularity with the *Terminator* film series (I and II directed by James Cameron, 1984 and 1991). It is not just about the future, when we look at the films, but our contemporary life, and our increased engagement with not just even intelligent machines, but things, products and tech devices we use frequently on a day-by-day basis. The way films like *Videodrome* have to cut deep with their abject scenes might be a way to break the ice more than anything else. The main thing is not futurism, but the uncanny side of the tech intruders that our life is full of – from artificial hearts to "borrowed" ones (heart surgeries have been made since 1967,[47] to the way we stare at screens.

Our interaction with tech is more somatic than intellectual. The intellectual side might be on the top of my aspiration to use a computer, but that side is not about interaction with the PC, which consists of my staring at the screen, my use of fingers, sitting at the computer and carrying it with me. Sometimes when I go to sleep I notice that my wrist hurts and my eyes can still see the light of the writing program.

The films that have portrayed fantasies of our engagements with machines, equipment and things have been sort of avant-garde, but in a special way, being mass art at the same time, and people not really noticing or reflecting upon their pioneering side that much. They have helped us to drag ourselves out from humanist metaphysics by letting us see a glimpse of what it might be to be just a thing, machine or an object, and so supported our often unconscious reflection of this type of experience in our everyday.

The way we receive, register and react on our couches is something that feels very natural, and maybe it is something that we in a way or another did already when we roamed the Savannah – maybe watched the glow of the fire in the evenings, or the stars. And the state of our minds and bodies, when we semi-hibernate in the evenings, when our kids have already gone to bed, might be something that Raymond Williams was already hinting upon in his remark that (I will here paraphrase): it is not important what you watch, it is about having the TV on or off.[48] Today we need to see this in a wider scope, not forgetting the Internet or any other technological mass media devices.

Interestingly this animalistic mode of semi-hibernating, not being active or reflective, might often feel more thingy than our activities with cars or team play in sports – because of the strong atmosphere that films are able to produce, and maybe the bodily reactions that we gain by watching these films. This is where Perniola's opening on the theme is so important. It stresses passivity, flexibility with, not resistance to, the technological and (object-driven) consumerist change we experience. It focuses on less-discussed ways of being active, and less-discussed as well as probably, at least so far less-appreciated, ways of feeling pleasure (about feeling cold, just like a thing, etc.).

The protagonist of Cronenberg's *Videodrome*, Max Renn (played by James Woods) shouts at the end of the movie, after radical body-mind, man-tech and man-machine transformations: "Long live the new flesh." It is of course a provocative thrill, uncanny slapstick, but as Walter Benjamin once thought that factory work, amusement parks, photography, fast-paced traffic and film have to change our perception (they changed for sure at least something in our experience, for sure), we have for long been forced to ask what the new world order is doing to us. We might also need new skills to separate ourselves from what we see and what we use (technologically), like we once needed to defend ourselves from the first new shocks of early twentieth-century technology and its applications (like montage, which even made people pass out as they were scared at the beginning of film history). But together with our culture of using the new technological equipment we have, we of course work out new ways of building aesthetic experience, too.

We might experience ourselves increasingly differently from the way people in the past did. But this of course does not affect our feeling of being real, whole human beings, at least not necessarily. We might, though, want to consider these oscillations discussed here, atmospheres, and even margins of experience, as something that exists and that we might need to cope with, at least at some point. We might have to accept that we enjoy sometimes feeling like things only, just machines, and becoming partly things with our increasingly techno-logical in-built equipment, from amalgam fillings to joint replace-ments, from drugs that change the working of the brain to glasses/spectacles, intelligent clothes (like a second skin) and the implants that the people working in high-tech companies and media labs (my own, Aalto Media Lab, counted in) keep saying will become part of our everyday in just a few years.

Back to the Heart

The story of Chopin's heart is way beyond reasonable. The sister of the composer, Ludwika Jędrzejewicz, heard her brother's wish to be dismembered – and took the request seriously. After preserving the heart of Chopin in something that is usually thought of as having been a cognac jar, which was then well sealed, she covered it with a more traditional mahogany/oak urn. She smuggled it to Poland.

And in 1879 the vessel found its home in the Church of the Holy Cross in Warsaw.

When the Germans came and Poland had to subdue to their regime, the heart was close to being totally lost, maybe forever. During the Warsaw Uprising there was much chaos and some serious battles around the area of the Church of the Holy Cross, and the building was even damaged to some extent. A German priest with the name Schulze approached then his local peers asking if they'd be interested in helping him to get the heart out of the city that was endangering it. This was agreed on, and Heinz Reinefarth, who was an SS officer, and also a friend of so called classical music and the work of the Polish composer, was the person who took the duty of finishing the process. The heart spent the rest of the uprising at the main base of Erich von dem Bach-Zelewski, who, paradoxically, was the infamous brutal commander of the Nazis in the Warsaw region.

What happens then is even more uncanny. The priests took the heart back after the uprising. They traveled with it to a small town called Milanówek, which lies in the vicinity of Warsaw. They were reflecting on the possibility that the invaders might suddenly change their way of thinking about the issue, so they did a good job by hiding it well in Milanówek. During this process, they had a look inside the container. They claimed that the heart of the composer was "incredibly big," as one onlooker had it. The heart was taken back to its original home October 17, 1945.

I love the story, as it is already in itself like a film – one that could be the end product of a process started by Roger Corman, David Cronenberg or Nicolas Roeg, all explorers of the uncanny side of humanity. The fetishizing of the dismembered heart, and the pathetic, but uncanny worship of artistic (male) genius (which might have been at its peak at the time[49]), build a bit of a disgusting, but at the same time dynamically interesting (this is the main feature of aesthetic disgust according to Aurel Kolnai[50]), tension. It leads us to the same kind of experience that we might get when we read about a weird and a bit disgusting plot of a film, but even more, it shows that our fantasies of the future or stories about phantasmatic parallel universes, where absurdist, uncanny things happen, are not that unrealistic, as our history is full of stories, old customs (as we saw in the beginning of the article in the discourse on dismemberments) and filmic episodes, which might actually, if we did not know the years of these events, sound like science fiction to us. There are countless ways we might develop our culture of tech and the mass cultures and mass arts that it facilitates. If philosophy and cultural studies have sometimes been a bit slow in following these intuitions, it is important to note that film has been testing the limits of the fantasies already for ages, and so they might have been doing more for our self-understanding. By mutilating bodies, intersecting humankind with other species and machines, so that our bodies react to it when we see it happening in filmic reality, creating soundscapes which turn our stomachs upside down, and stories that extend both our feelings of disgust and pleasure, they have also for sure supported our reflection on our new companion techs (which are like companion species – to hear pay tribute to Donna Haraway[51]), and the possible futures for our "new flesh." We cannot study the future, but we can study these experiences. Where do our experiences of being one-on-one with animals, machines, tech and just things, in this world, where their presence is felt more than ever, lead us? Experiences do not lie, but to make something out of them, we also need to reflect on them philosophically. To some extent they are the best mirrors we have for discussing the tactile and the not yet that much reachable. We need to listen to our bodies more.

Conclusions

Experiencing the body to be a machine and "just" or partly a thing might not be dominant, but it is a contemporary phenomenon we should study if we desire to understand contemporary experience. Films both stimulate and help to analyze this experience. We might have to push aside some of our holistic and humanist dreams to reach a new understanding of ourselves as partly inorganic and partly being invaded by the world of commodities. This does not have to be only negative, though, and I hope that this text would help us to look at the potentials of our changing experience in a changing world.

Notes

1 A bit in America too. See, for example, the article on James Lindsay's, Helen Pluckrose's and Peter Boghossian's work which aims to show how "postmodenist" theory is not in the end critical. Yascha Mounk, "What an Audacious Hoax Reveals About Academia," *The Atlantic*, October 5, 2018. https://www.theatlantic.com/ideas/archive/2018/10/new-sokal-hoax/572212/. Last accessed: Dec 9, 2021.
2 See, for example, bell hooks, "Postmodern Blackness," *Yearning: Race, Gender and Cultural Politics* (New York – London: Routledge, 2015), 23–32. See also Sonya Lindfors, ed, *Blackness & the Postmodern* (Helsinki: UrbanApa, 2018).

3 See, for example, Tate's definition (accessed 17.11.2021) "Body Art" (Art Terms): http://www.tate.org.uk/art/art-terms/b/body-art.

4 See, for example, Jean-Luc Nancy, *Corpus* (New York: Fordham University Press, 2008) and Luce Irigaray, *Between East and West: From Singularity to Community* (New York: Columbia University Press, 2003).

5 For philosophical notes on this, see, for example, Richard Shusterman, *Thinking through the Body*.

6 See, for example, Jukka Sihvonen, *Aivokuvia* (Turku: Eetos, 2013) and Erkki Huhtamo, "From Cybernation to Interaction: A Contribution to an Archeology of Interactivity," in *The Digital Dialectic: New Essays on New Media*, ed. Peter Lunenfeld, 96–110 (Cambridge, Mass.: The MIT Press, 1999).

7 Linda Williams, "Film Bodies: Gender, Genre, and Excess."

8 Carol J. Clover, "Her Body, Himself: Gender in the Slasher Film."

9 This position is taken and defended by Hermann Broch. Hermann Broch, "Das Böse im Wertsystem der Kunst," in *Texte Zur Nietsche-Rezeption 1873–1963*, ed. B. Hillebrand (Berlin: De Gruyter, 1968).

10 I am here following the micro-historical work of Steven Lagerberg. *Chopin's Heart: The Quest to Identify the Mysterious Illness of the World's Most Beloved Composer* (Scotts Valley: Create Space, 2011).

11 For the whole (global) history of heart-extraction, see Armin Dietz, *Ewige Herzen: Kleine Kulturgeschichte der Herzbestattungen* (Munich: Medien & Medizin Verlag, 1998).

12 Dietz, *Ewige Herzen*, 105–115.

13 Dietz, *Ewige Herzen*,123–147.

14 See, for example, Stahl Stenslie, "Stelarc: On The Body as an Artistic Material," *The Journal of Somaesthetics* 1 (2015): 1, 20–41.

15 Gaius Julius Caesar, *De bello gallico*. Found, for example, at Gutenberg: http://www.gutenberg.org/ebooks/10657.

16 See my critique of this: Max Ryynänen, "Throwing the Body into the Fight: The Body as an Instrument in Political Art," *The Journal of Somaesthetics* 1 (2015): 108–121.

17 https://sugarcanemag.com/2020/06/how-to-engage-in-healing-by-viewing-black-contemporary-art-by-chenoa-baker/

18 Gilles Deleuze and Felix Guattari, *Anti-Oedipus* (Minneapolis: University of Minnesota Press, 1983), 1.

19 Mario Perniola, *Il Sex Appeal dell'inorganico* (Torino: Einaudi, 2004).

20 Mario Perniola, *Contro comunicazione* (Torino: Einaudi, 2004), 14.

21 Laura Mulvey, "Visual Pleasure and Narrative Cinema," *Screen* 16, no. 3 (1976): 6–18.

22 Wendy Steiner's take on the way females keep competing males in a test-laboratory situation, while they compete for the female gaze, is a great take on the topic. See Wendy Steiner, "The Beauty of Choice: Aesthetics and the Agency of Women," in *Companion to Aesthetics and its Companions*, ed. Max Ryynänen & Zoltan Somhegyi (London: Rowman & Littlefield, forthcoming).

23 See, for example, Karl Max, *Capital* (London: Penguin Classics, 1990), 165.

24 In Erica Sherover, "The Virtue of Poverty: Marx's Transformation of Hegel's Concept of the Poor," *Canadian Journal of Political and Social Theory* 3, no 1 (Winter 1979): 57.

25 Ibid, 58.
26 Ibid, 58.
27 Ibid., 59.
28 Ibid.
29 For the debate in full 1842, see, for example, ttps://marxists.architexturez.net/archive/marx/works/1842/10/25.htm#n1.
30 More on this, see Jacques Rancière, *The Philosopher and His Poor* (Durham: Duke University Press, 2004).
31 Walter Benjamin (ed. Beatrice Hanssen), *Walter Benjamin and the Arcades Project* (London: Continuum, 2006), 71.
32 These thoughts form the base of *The Writer of Modern Life* (Cambridge: Harvard University Press, 2006).
33 I here of course pay homage to Donna Haraway.
34 Martin Heidegger, *Discourse on Thinking* (New York: Harper Torch Books, 1966).
35 Jacques Rancière, *Proletarian Nights: The Worker's Dream in Nineteenth-Century France* (London: Verso, 2012).
36 Jacques Rancière, *The Ignorant Schoolmaster. Five Lessons in Intellectual Emancipation* (Stanford: Stanford University Press, 1991). See especially pages 8–18.
37 See my and Jozef Kovalcik's short introduction to Adorno's popular culture theory in "A History of the Aesthetics of Popular Culture," in *Aesthetics of Popular Culture*, edited by Jozef Kovalcik and Max Ryynänen, 14–49 (Bratislava: Slovart, 2014).
38 Guy Debord, *Society of the Spectacle* (Detroit: Black and Red, 1970).
39 Jacques Rancière, *The Emancipated Spectator* (London: Verso, 2009).
40 See, for example, Erkki Huhtamo, ed., *Sähköiho: Kone, media, ruumis* (Tampere: Vastapaino, 1995). Nicholas Negroponte's vision of virtual reality was very enthusiastic, too. Driving schools still do not work with VR, partly for the reason, that it is more efficient (and cheaper) to just drive. One extra thing could be also the fact that driving is quite somatic, so it is good to do with the body in a real context. Nicholas Negroponte, *Being Digital* (London: Hodder & Stoughton, 1995), 117.
41 Carroll however also talks critically about this "protestant ethics of aesthetics." See Noël Carroll, *A Philosophy of Mass Art* (Clarendon: Oxford University Press, 1998), 48.
42 Samir Gandesha and Jonathan Hartle, "Introduction," in *Aesthetic Marx*, ed. Samir Gandesha and Jonathan Hartle (New York: Bloomsbury, 2017).
43 Theodor Adorno, "Culture Industry: Enlightenment as Mass Deception," in *Dialectics of Enlightenment: Philosophical Fragments* (Stanford: Stanford University Press, 2002).
44 This was one novelty of Brentano's 1874 work: Franz Brentano, *Psychology from an Empirical Standpoint* (London: Routledge, 1995), and famously had an impact on, for example, his student's Sigmund Freud's thinking.
45 Carole Talon-Hugon, *Goût et dégoût: L'art peut-il tout montrer?* (Nice: Actes Sud, 2003).
46 Henry Parland, *To Pieces* (London: Norvik Press, 2011).
47 Dietz, *Ewige Herzen*, 149.

48 Raymond Williams, *Technology and Cultural* Form (New York: Schocken Books, 1975), 86, 93.
49 Christine Battersby, *Gender and Genius: Towards a Feminist Aesthetics* (London: The Women's Press, 1989).
50 Aurel Kolnai, "Disgust," in *On Disgust: Edited and with an Introduction by Barry Smith and Carolyn Korsmeyer* (Chicago: Open Court, 2004).
51 Donna Haraway, *The Companion Species Manifesto: Dogs, People, and Significant Otherness* (Chicago: Chicago University Press, 2003).

Bibliography

Adorno, Theodor, and Max Horkheimer. "Culture Industry: Enlightenment as Mass Deception." In *Dialectics of Enlightenment: Philosophical Fragments*, 94–136. Stanford: Stanford University Press, 2002.

Battersby, Christine. *Gender and Genius: Towards a Feminist Aesthetics*. London: The Women's Press, 1989.

Benjamin, Walter. *Walter Benjamin and the Arcades Project*, edited by Beatrice Hanssen. London: Continuum, 2006.

Benjamin, Walter. "The Work of Art in the Age of its Technological Reproducibility." In *The Work of Art in the Age of its Technological Reproducibility and Other Writings on Media*, edited by M. Jennings, B. Doherty, and T. Levin, 19–55. Cambridge, MA: The Belknap Press of Harvard University Press, 2008.

Brentano, Franz. *Psychology from an Empirical Standpoint*. London: Routledge, 1995.

Broch, Hermann. "Das Böse im Wertsystem der Kunst." In *Texte Zur Nietsche-Rezeption 1873–1963*, edited by B. Hillebrand, 49–76. Berlin: De Gryuter, 1968.

Caesar, Gaius Julius. *De bello gallico*. Gutenberg: http://www.gutenberg.org/ebooks/10657.

Carroll, Noël. *A Philosophy of Mass Art*. Clarendon: Oxford University Press, 1998.

Deleuze, Gilles, and Felix Guattari. *Anti-Oedipus*. Minneapolis: University of Minnesota Press, 1983.

Dietz, Armin. *Ewige Herzen: Kleine Kulturgeschichte der Herzbestattungen*. Munich: Medien & Medizin Verlag, 1998.

Gandesha, Samir, and Jonathan Hartle. "Introduction." In *Aesthetic Marx*, edited by Samir Gandesha and Jonathan Hartle. New York: Bloomsbury, 2017.

Haraway, Donna. *The Companion Species Manifesto: Dogs, People, and Significant Otherness*. Chicago: Chicago University Press, 2003.

Heidegger, Martin. *Discourse on Thinking*. New York: Harper Torch Books, 1966.

hooks, bell. "Postmodern Blackness." In *Yearning: Race, Gender and Cultural Politics*, 23–31. New York – London: Routledge, 2015.

Huhtamo, Erkki, ed., *Sähköiho: Kone, media, ruumis.* Tampere: Vastapaino, 1995.

Huhtamo, Erkki. "From Cybernation to Interaction: A Contribution to an Archeology of Interactivity." In *The Digital Dialectic: New Essays on New Media*, edited by Peter Lunenfeld, 96–110. Cambridge, Mass: The MIT Press, 1999.

Irigaray, Luce. *Between East and West: From Singularity to Community.* New York: Columbia University Press, 2003.

Kolnai, Aurel. "Disgust." In *On Disgust: Edited and with an Introduction by Barry Smith and Carolyn Korsmeyer.* Chicago: Open Court, 2004.

Kovalcik, Jozef, and Max Ryynänen, "A History of the Aesthetics of Popular Culture," In *Aesthetics of Popular Culture*, edited by Jozef Kovalcik and Max Ryynänen, 14–49. Bratislava: Slovart, 2014.

Lagerberg, Steven. *Chopin's Heart: The Quest to Identify the Mysterious Illness of the World's Most Beloved Composer.* Scotts Valley: Create Space, 2011.

Lindfors, Sonya, ed., *Blackness & the Postmodern.* Helsinki: UrbanApa, 2018.

Marx, Karl. *Capital.* London: Penguin Classics, 1990.

Mounk, Yascha."What an Audacious Hoax Reveals About Academia." *The Atlantic*, October 5, 2018. https://www.theatlantic.com/ideas/archive/2018/10/new-sokal-hoax/572212/. Last accessed: Dec 9, 2021.

Mulvey, Laura. "Visual Pleasure and Narrative Cinema." *Screen* 16, no. 3 (1976): 6–18.

Nancy, Jean-Luc. *Corpus.* New York: Fordham University Press, 2008.

Negroponte, Nicholas. *Being Digital.* London: Hodder & Stoughton, 1995.

Parland, Henry. *To Pieces.* London: Norvik Press, 2011.

Perniola, Mario. *Contro comunicazione.* Torino: Einaudi, 2004.

Perniola, Mario. *Il Sex Appeal dell'inorganico.* Torino: Einaudi, 2004.

Rancière, Jacques. *The Ignorant Schoolmaster. Five Lessons in Intellectual Emancipation.* Stanford: Stanford University Press, 1991.

Rancière, Jacques. *The Philosopher and His Poor.* Durham: Duke University Press, 2004.

Rancière, Jacques. *The Emancipated Spectator.* London: Verso, 2009.

Rancière, Jacques. *Proletarian Nights: The Worker's Dream in Nineteenth-Century France.* London: Verso, 2012.

Ryynänen, Max. "Throwing the Body into the Fight: The Body as an Instrument in Political Art." *The Journal of Somaesthetics* 1 (2015): 108–121.

Sherover, Erica. "The Virtue of Poverty: Marx's Transformation of Hegel's Concept of the Poor." *Canadian Journal of Political and Social Theory* 3, no. 1 (Winter 1979): 53–66.

Shusterman, Richard. *Thinking Through the Body.* Cambridge: Cambridge University Press, 2012.

Sihvonen, Jukka. *Aivokuvia.* Turku: Eetos, 2013.

Steiner, Wendy. "The Beauty of Choice: Aesthetics and the Agency of Women." In *Companion to Aesthetics and its Companions*, edited by Max Ryynänen and Zoltan Somhegyi. London: Rowman & Littlefield, Forthcoming, 2023.

Stenslie, Stahl. "Stelarc: On The Body as an Artistic Material." *The Journal of Somaesthetics* 1 (2015): 20–41.

Talon-Hugon, Carole. *Goût et dégoût: L'art peut-il tout montrer?* Nice: Actes Sud, 2003.

Williams, Linda. "Film Bodies: Gender, Genre, and Excess." *Film Quarterly* 44, no. 4 (Summer, 1991): 2–13.

Williams, Raymond. *Technology and Cultural Form.* New York: Schocken Books, 1975.

4 Robot Cars

Our worldview owes a lot to science – but when it rains, we do not experience H2O or the "physical particles" that constitute rain. This is something phenomenologists have invited us to understand since the 1920s. The mindset of the "European" (today more or less, the people of the World) might fundamentally lean on natural science, as Edmund Husserl concluded,[1] but when it rains, we hear, see and feel *rain* – the phenomenon.

For the people of today, cars are like rain. Witnessing the glow of the endless stream of vehicles on the New Jersey Turnpike near Newark at dawn or the dusty chain of metal on the crossroads of Via delle Catene and the ancient Via Aurelia (241 BC) on a sunny Saturday morning is analogous to watching falling rain or burning logs in a fireplace. Even if we *know* that the car consists of a metal shell (however electronic they might become, it still creates an environmental problem[2]), the motor, exterior and interior design with modern textiles and plastic parts, and still at least one human being, this is not the way we always perceive them in the everyday stream of consciousness and experience. The accent changes with the context, of course. Sometimes it's grandmother. Sometimes it's a Mercedes. The car and its driver, passengers and the items that it carries, are both one and differentiated in the experience.

The history of modern traffic is long enough for the experience of cars to become "natural" but even less history would be enough for this experience – as we know from the fast naturalization of our experience of cell phones. Cars are a part of our lifeworld (*Lebenswelt*), the self-evident and/or given (to discuss it via Edmund Husserl's thinking), the great platform where "(w)e, as living in wakeful world-consciousness, are constantly active on the basis of our passive having of the world." Or, to (take the paragraph as whole, and to) take a more social approach:

DOI: 10.4324/9781003248514-4

In whatever way we may be conscious of the world as universal horizon, as coherent universe of existing objects, we, each "I-the-man" and all of us together, belong to the world as living with one another in the world; and the world is our world, valid for our consciousness as existing precisely through this "living together." We, as living in wakeful world-consciousness, are constantly active on the basis of our passive having of the world... Obviously this is true not only for me, the individual ego; rather we, in living together, have the world pre-given in this together, belong, the world as world for all, pre-given with this ontic meaning.[3]

Although Husserl noted the complexity of the human-animal relationship/difference and although there might have been "hesitant attempts to extend personhood to animals" in his thinking (as Mario Vergani nails it[4]) his "we-subjectivity" embraced only human beings while even animals remained as extreme otherness, although, good to note, in Husserl's later writings he accentuated that there were "degrees of subjectivity" which has invited some philosophers to ask if his philosophy actually entails an opening to discuss inter-subjectivity (with animals).[5]

When it comes to cars (or other increasingly "smart" devices) as handy tools for us, Husserl's philosophy does not offer much. He eventually made notes on (e.g. useful) things in his "Renewal: Its Problem and Method" (originally published between 1923–1924), where he discusses humanity as a subject of culture, commodities (*Gut*) and accomplishments.[6] According to Husserl, only man produces commodities and gives them a role in an aspiration to become immortal. His comments came close to Martin Heidegger's idea of readiness-to-hand[7] (Heidegger had already talked about this topic in 1919). Husserl's thinking was more fragmented and less developed than that of his student (Heidegger), but he saw broader problematics in our daily things, from life to death.

Heidegger's thinking provides other openings, though. When cars are old, particularly beautiful ones, or when they drive so fast that we react, and even more if they have crashed, they are present-at-hand (*Vorhandenheit*). Mostly however, they are just ready-to-hand (*Zuhandenheit*) tools/equipment, like hammers.

The less we just stare at the hammer-thing, and the more we seize hold of it and use it, the more primordial does our relationship to it become, and the more unveiledly is it encountered as that which it is—as equipment. The hammering itself uncovers the specific "manipulability" of the hammer. The kind of Being which equipment possesses—in which it manifests itself in its own right—we call "readiness-to-hand."[8]

Heidegger wants to say that, in a way, the tool disappears in its functionality, following its everyday nature and reliability. When one uses a hammer, one is not looking at it as one looks at an object, but through engagement, an engagement that connects to the cultural system, and actually an entire network of equipment/tools, one does not deal with a position vis-à-vis the world of objects. It becomes, in a sense, transparent. We notice its role/meaning mainly when it is broken.

Hammers are not central for our contemporary digital lifestyle and neither are saws or needles (Heidegger's other examples of equipment/ tools), but it is not hard to understand and somehow connect to Heidegger's description of the network of equipment/tools that keep the wheels of our life turning: "equipment for writing, sewing, working, transportation, measurement."[9] In *Being and Time* he also mentions the turn signals of an automobile.

I've already noted how the endless flow of cars can feel as natural as rain. When we hear the flow of traffic from our windows, we don't even think of individual cars, in the same way that we do not think of individual rain drops or the chemical code of rain ($H2O$). But then, as shown above, cars can be like hammers. Our lifestyle is very much based upon our use of them. And using them is craft. One presses the gas pedal, shifts gears, uses the windscreen wipers and turns the wheel, gazes closely at what happens and moves the ton of metal through landscapes. As Maurice Merleau-Ponty first showed in philosophical discourse, man disappears in his/her extensions and becomes one with the car – as much as his/her clothes, rings and tools.[10] When one turns the wheel, one moves an extended self, a bulk of a body. In light of Mario Perniola's philosophy, one could put it another way: through our extensive use of technological devices, avatars, things and tools, we also increasingly experience ourselves as "just" things. Allegorically speaking, tools may become invisible to us, but our feeling of toolness becomes a norm. The car sneaks into us.

In J.G. Ballard's *Crash* (1973), a book that one can read either as a dystopia of the effects of the extensive use of cars on us, or a hypothetical fantasy about a new car-driven sexuality and cultural experience, cars inevitably take over – first psychologically, but then also physically. The protagonist/narrator James Ballard meets Dr. Robert Vaughan as a result of a car accident close to London Airport. A small network of alienated, lost souls who have experienced car-crashes and who have developed a form of sexual fetishism for them become their community. They have fantasies of celebrities having car-crashes. And they produce some deliberately.

> "At first I aimlessly followed the perimeter roads to the south of the airport, feeling out the unfamiliar controls among the water reservoirs of Stanwell. From here I moved around the eastern flank of the airport to the motorway interchanges at Harlington, where the rush-hour traffic leaving London swept me back in a huge tidal race of metal along the crowded lanes of Western Avenue."[11]

Crash is a sensual vision of what life might become, one that is quite easy to understand if one remembers how much the production and use of cars has accelerated throughout the years. For example, in 1960, the US there were 62 million registered cars, but by 1995 that number had risen to 128 million – and today the amount is close to 300 million. The end of the 1970s marked the time when traffic control was slowly taking over, but when it was still much more dangerous to drive than it is today. The number of traffic-related deaths in many countries was 3 to 4 times higher than it is today.[12]

Today we face new phases of development. Like all generations, we are on the road to a world we do not yet know. In 1959, Heidegger wrote the following in his *Discourse on Thinking*:

> What we know now as the technology of film and television, of transportation and especially air transportation, of news reporting, and as medical and nutritional technology, is presumably only a crude start. No one can foresee the radical changes to come.[13]

Our time, I think, is the time of robotics – and our increasing turn from sci-fi fantasies and questions about their intelligence to practical experience and comments on being with them.

My campus at Aalto University has featured test cars which have been driving around, functioning as buses, since 2015. They are not beautiful in the sense reserved for design objects, but different and curiosity raising. They are aesthetically stimulating as objects, at least slightly, but even more, they force us to face another way of coping with cars, as there is no driver, sometimes not even passengers – just one student making sure that the car does not make "human" or "inhuman" mistakes.

At first, I was afraid of the robot cars, but after 18 months of watching how slowly, carefully and sensitively they drive, I felt safer than ever. When I walked out from my workplace and a robot car was approaching, it slowed down and I started to feel cared for.

Of course, a team of people worked out how the car reacts, and what kind of sensors it uses, what patterns it follows, without forgetting that new technology is able to "learn" in new situations; but still, this is how humans function too, as we are trained, filled with knowledge, educational patterns and propaganda, and ultimately, if someone reacts to you and follows your moves, it is pleasant, as long as you know he/she/it is not programmed to harm you.

It all boils down to an individual that I saw speeding away in his car just a couple of meters from the house where I was working. He was tired, dumb, aggressive, and stressed, and as he gazed at his cell phone, he drove faster and more dangerously. At that moment I realized that this was the programming I was afraid of, the aggressive masculinity that did not care for others. I had to reflect on thinking that sometimes, I felt something, which in a very marginal way was like care or a new form of sympathy (still based on the old forms), when I met the robot car, but all communication, all interaction, went out the window when I saw the sweaty office worker on his way home. He probably cared more than I could feel for the people he might hit and was just tired, while the robot car did not "care" at all intentionally speaking, but they acted differently, and acts sometimes make us react more than intentions. When one thinks of it, a friendly psychopath with no empathy still raises our sympathy if we get pleasant treatment (and we often do not recognize the psycho among us). Although the human driver of my example might wake up mentally and ethically after an accident, the modality he possessed was raw, unethical and without concern for other beings. And when I thought of his brain, where his model of behavior had been planted, where the traits of his "training" had formed connections, where neuron networks helped him to navigate through life as much as traffic, and where his body pumped blood through a technically complicated, but quite automated organ called the heart, I could no longer separate him from his car extensions and the robot car.

Interestingly, unlike in the typical film and AI discussion-wise fantasy of talking with an Alien or communicating with a robot, my communication existed only visually and somatically. My pleasure arose from interaction, and even more, from my vision that marked the interaction in the robot car's movements, and its "consciousness" about me being there, to care for me the way it had been designed to do. Although the robot car was first present-at-hand very visibly, it became a sort of an agent in my close environment something that was about readiness-to-hand in the way Heidegger discussed it. Although I felt more like being *with it*, than being with the stressed-up male driving his car (not noticing me in any way), and this being with increased through my somatic feeling that the robot car reacted to me and cared for me, at the same time it became like just another tool or piece of equipment among others in my daily flow, one that I could trust like the coffee maker or my own car. A companion machine, a companion in traffic caring for me – through deeds.

As robot cars move slowly, softly and attentively, I feel that my body is safe, and the dialogue with them, which is half about vision and half about somatics, can provide pleasure (although I know the robot does not have a body like me, but owns a different kind of moving body, a bit like a spider or an ant).

We have overrated the radicalness of robots in everyday life, not just in science fiction but also in many studies conducted in the past. Why did we not realize that as we could feel some sort of compassion for an old car that had served us well, we might, in the same way start feeling even more compassion for machines that somehow notice us, i.e. robots? Of course, the issue extends well beyond tech. We don't see tombstones as just stones; they are in some sense "living matter" as Elisabeth Povinelli notes, and most of us wouldn't like to sleep in a room with a tombstone. Povinelli's *Geontologies: A Requiem to Late Liberalism* (2016) touches on issues like environmentalism, where understanding how non-living objects in a sense are at times living matter for us, and how understanding the degree to which the material base our bodies shares with some geological sites can help us to see ourselves as less detached from nature. She talks about the sacred stones to which Australia's indigenous people tell their problems. As people have done that for thousands of years, and as we are afraid of tombstones and yet somehow feel the presence of Elvis Presley's comb (like a magical object), how on earth can we be so suspect of our future affective and emotional relationship with robots, which ultimately have many more human features than the examples mentioned here? Belief systems do a lot, but so do interactions, as in my example; somatic interaction produces much more than intellectual interaction.

Quite fast in everyday life (this is what I've noticed), like tombstones, robot-driven cars oscillate between being slightly alive (and with us) and not alive. For phenomenology and somaesthetics this calls for attention. In *Being and Time* (1927) Heidegger wrote about how being-with (*Mitsein*, with people) was central for our Being, an ineliminable part of what we are – a part of we, not just me, in a way that is perhaps also hard to distinguish at times.[14] But in the same way that recent studies on material culture have understood how objects, things and equipment are central for us and culture, although we haven't gone so far as to start talking about them as a part of being-with, robots might extend the questioning to some sort of being in our conception and at least the tacit feeling of "we." Dogs have done it, and those who have a turtle or a spider at home, experience it – if not as strongly, then at least to some respect. And although I saw the robot car every day as a machine, as tech, and experienced it as a piece of equipment/tool of some kind (even if I did not use it), I also felt a marginal sense of mutuality with it, maybe something tacit and not that clear, but still, something.

One thing is certain. Our phenomenological field, where we take note of human beings, animals, plants, and rocks, will surely be challenged, and it is hard to say where, taxonomically speaking, we will place robotic objects which will increasingly accompany us. The problem might lie in our overly simple taxonomies, and the fact that we don't yet rely on our somatic instincts regarding who we are *with* and how. They still form the base for our daily experience of *Mitseins* of all sorts. Also, in art, where robots have been trendy and present for long, seeing robots do things or understanding their intelligence, does not yet raise as much feeling as engaging somatically with them. Although seeing e-David paint with artist Liat Grayver on film raises awe,[15] engaging with the same artist's robots in sand in *Open Close Open* in the Jewish Museum Berlin (2019) really felt like something.[16]

Countless books have recently addressed this problematic of being transhuman,[17] but they mostly focus on robots and cyborgs through their consciousness, not as partners of somatic interaction. The persona, personal identity, or whatever, might not be something I think about when I meet a spider (which I react to physically) more than a robot. The way human beings might lose their Vitruvian role as the center for consciousness might, in the end, not be the issue, but with what and how we interact, as our body does a lot of work in inhabituating machines. To inhabituate a factory machine might be hard in the way Charlies Chaplin showed in his *Modern Times* (1936), where as, the protagonist, he went into the factory machinery and became fed with the help of an uncanny machine; but today's tech is something else. For someone experiencing it, its "IQ" might be uninteresting, but its interaction with the mind-body, builds the relationship and the feeling for it. We have underestimated the soma. Are we entering a moment of truth in our encounter with technology, where we will understand ourselves better through the new everyday dialogue with robotics, where the soma leads the development? This dialogue might be adding more depth to our encounters with robots, than any knowledge or experience of their level of intelligence. Like the living and reflective soma that no longer feels awed by the strong smell of gasoline, the loud noise made by fossil engines, or the unreliable, insufficiently trained/computed driver, it thinks as little about the intelligence of the machines it spends time with as it sits thinking about the IQ of the salesmen or bus drivers it meets (without even thinking about dogs and spiders). It is the somatic interaction which will predicate the future of sex robots, not our knowledge about their persona or IQ. This will be *the* question for whom we feel being with, as the intelligent machines also become increasingly agile, flexible, and softer at some point, more like us, or the creatures with whom we have become accustomed to extending our communication and interaction, like dogs and cats, that are programmed with much more genetic information than we, who receive a lot culturally, being programmed in a different way.

Daniel White and Hirofumi Katsuno (2021) studied the affective relationship to robots by taking a look at "a memorial service for 109 pet robots" in Japan, where the priest claimed that one needs to put aside the theoretical, discursive assumptions about life and focus on the sense. When one looks at what matters to people, things are not logical in a rationalist way. The sense of life is what matters, and it can extend anywhere, as we, human beings of a culture, take part in cultivating it. However, we can't necessarily choose what we desire to sense life in. It all seems to crave a new research agenda, White and Katsuno have written a "somatic toolkit" for anthropology.[18] While not providing it in their study, I have attempted to provide a framework for understanding the topic with the help of some somaesthetic notes. But although developing these thoughts to their utmost, theoretical thinking is not enough. I might just need to live through the robotic revolution to feel it, and thus, understand more.

Conclusions

Machines are programmed, but so are we – with, for example, knowledge, ideologies and somatic practices. Robot cars might in this sense not be as different from human-driven cars than what we have so far imagined. Interaction with robots makes their intelligence anyway a side issue. We build our relationship to robots through visual and somatic engagement and dialogue. To learn from our bodies when they meet robots, might be one of the most important paths for understanding our relationship to new technology.

Notes

1 Edmund Husserl, *The Crisis of European Sciences and Transcendental Philosophy* (Cambridge: Cambridge University Press, 2012).
2 I am thankful to Tere Vadén for this note.
3 Husserl, Edmund, *The Crisis of the European Sciences*, 108–109.
4 Mario Vergani, "Husserl's Hesitant Attempts to Extend Personhood to Animals," *Husserl Studies*, 28 April, 2020, note 6.
5 See Jean-Claude Monod, "Why I Talk to My Dog," *Environmental Philosophy* 11, No. 1 (Spring 2014): 17–26.
6 Edmund Husserl, "Erneuerung als individualethisches Problem," in *Aufsätze und Vorträge (1922–1937), Husserliana Gesammelte Werke, Band XXVII*, edited by T. Nenon and H.R. Sepp, 20–43 (Haag: Kluwer Academic Publishers, 1988).
7 Tom Nenon, "Freedom, Responsibility, and Self-Awareness in Husserl," in *The New Yearbook for Phenomenology and Phenomenological Philosophy 2*, edited by Burt Hopkins and Steven Crowell, 1–21. New York: Routledge, 2002.
8 Martin Heidegger, *Being and Time* (Oxford: Blackwell, 1962), 98.
9 Heidegger, *Being and Time*, 97.
10 Maurice Merleau-Ponty, *Phenomenology of Perception* (New Yok: Humanities Press, 1962).
11 J.G. Ballard, *Crash* (London: Fourth Estate, 2011), 6–7.
12 See, for example, car statistics on Statista.com: https://www.statista.com/statistics/183505/number-of-vehicles-in-the-united-states-since-1990/.
13 Heidegger, *Discourse on Thinking*, 51.
14 Maybe Indo-European languages stress too much individuality? It might be useful to turn to, for example, Korean, where "we" is more central than "I." See, for example, Hye Young-Kim, *We as Self: Ouri, Intersubjectivity, and Presubjectivity* (Lanham: Lexington Books, 2021).
15 See, for example, Liat Grayver's webpage for material: https://www.liatgrayver.com/liat-grayver-about.
16 See the presentation of this award-winning exhibition: https://www.liatgrayver.com/open-closed-open.
17 See, for example, Aleksandra Łukaszewicz Alcaraz's *Are Cyborgs Persons? An Account for Futurist Ethics* (New York: Palgrave MacMillan, 2020).
18 Daniel White and Hirofumi Katsuno, "Toward an Affective Sense of Life: Artificial Intelligence, Animacy, and Amusement at a Robot Pet Memorial Service in Japan," *Cultural Anthropology* 36, Issue 2 (2021): 222–251. See especially pages 236, 242, and 245.

Bibliography

Ballard, J.G. *Crash*. London: Fourth Estate, 2011.

Heidegger, Martin. *Being and Time*. Oxford: Blackwell, 1962.

Heidegger, Martin. *Discourse on Thinking*. New York: Harper Torch Books, 1966.

Husserl, Edmund. "Erneuerung als individualethisches Problem." In *Aufsätze und Vorträge (1922–1937), Husserliana Gesammelte Werke, Band XXVII*, edited by T. Nenon and H.R. Sepp, 20–43. Haag: Kluwer Academic Publishers, 1988.

Husserl, Edmund. *The Crisis of European Sciences and Transcendental Philosophy*. Cambridge: Cambridge University Press, 2012.

Łukaszewicz Alcaraz, Aleksandra. *Are Cyborgs Persons? An Account for Futurist Ethics*. New York: Palgrave MacMillan. 2020.

Nenon, Tom. "Freedom, Responsibility, and Self-Awareness in Husserl." In *The New Yearbook for Phenomenology and Phenomenological Philosophy 2*, edited by Burt Hopkins and Steven Crowell (2002). 1–21. Routledge: New York.

Povinelli, Elisabeth. *Geontologies: A Requiem to Late Liberalism*. Durham: Duke University Press, 2016.

Vergani, Mario. "Husserl's Hesitant Attempts to Extend Personhood to Animals." *Husserl Studies*, 28 (April 2020): 67–83.

White, Daniel, and Hirofumi Katsuno. "Toward an Affective Sense of Life: Artificial Intelligence, Animacy, and Amusement at a Robot Pet Memorial Service in Japan." *Cultural Anthropology* 36, no. 2 (2021): 222–251.

Young-Kim, Hye. *We as Self: Ouri, Intersubjectivity, and Presubjectivity*. Lanham: Lexington Books, 2021.

5 Disgust, the Inorganic, and the Enigmatic: The Dank Media Philosophy of Mario Perniola

Mario Perniola's *Enigmas: The Egyptian Moment in Society and Art* (1995) might look like a call for getting rid of the ego, and less ego might also be one of the particles needed to embody the idea of the book, but there is more to it.

> A philosophy of the present is [...] an enigmatic philosophy. Nor could it be otherwise, given that present-day society is itself enigmatic. [...] The philosopher is precisely someone who turns him- or herself into nothing in order to listen to the present and all its enigmas, the person who silences his or her own desires, his or her own untidy affections and his or her own deeply held opinions in order to avoid placing obstacles and misleading screens in the way of an understanding of history's manifestations.[1]

It is, naturally, about the juxtaposition needed from philosophers, which Richard Rorty has well coined in his "Philosophy as Spectatorship and Participation."[2] To become a professional philosopher, one needs to turn into a spectator, so that one can gaze at things from a distance. In the end – here Rorty the meta-philosopher wakes up – one also needs to become a sort of spectator of philosophy.[3] The constant struggle to not become an insensitive, too-detached onlooker, and to neither lose the distance needed, so that one can continue making judgments and analyses about the seen, and building arguments without inverting to too many subjective points of view and one's own affects, is the key challenge.

Philosophy, in both Rorty's and Perniola's case, is, of course, a broader idea than the narrow academic conception of it – and extends to, for example, literature studies and cultural studies. Although Rorty claims that all interest in philosophy starts with ethics, he coins his role of the philosopher "aesthetic," as the spectator's role in a sense is

DOI: 10.4324/9781003248514-5

about looking with intellectual awe on what's happening around oneself.[4] But in Perniola's case, becoming a philosopher of the contemporary age craves for pushing one step further beyond spectatorship and analysis.

After a long history of (read again, broadly) philosophy's alliances with agencies like the Enlightenment, (German) idealism and Marxism, which had become invisible, but strong structures and ties for academics,[5] it was now time to break some of that web that kept philosophy as its captive, Perniola wrote.

Perniola's peer from the Torino school (whose most famous representative is Umberto Eco), Gianni Vattimo, had in 1983 edited a groundbreaking volume with Pier Aldo Rovatti, called *Pensiero debole* (*Weak Thinking*, 1983), where the authors claim that the changes we at the time were mostly packaging with the theoretical matrix "postmodernity" were not much actually about a radical breaking of ties with modernity, which many theorists were celebrating, but about a sort of weakening of the impact of the classifications and metaphysics (development, freedom, etc.) of modernity, which made their structures and effect more like regulative horizons for culture, something that we could not easily get rid of, something, which still somehow guided action, although less and less. It might be that we already dropped, a long time ago, some of the most banal, idealist ideas of objectivity, but still, objectivity is still somehow aspired to, even in humanities, and although religion no longer offered fundamental bricks to stand on in life, people have followed it in a shallower way in the West and the Global North.[6]

Vattimo's idea of "weakness," which, of course, as a concept was provocative, leaning toward, for example, impotence, was, though, not a good one, according to Perniola. He said, too, that "post-modernity essentially distinguishes itself from modernity only to the extent that it does not make any radical break therefrom!"[7] – and, for sure, he must have been inspired by the very local version of postmodern thinking that prevailed in Italy at the time. But when Vattimo interviewed Perniola in 1990, the latter attacked the word "weak" that Vattimo had used, claiming that the concept implied that modernity had somehow been based on strong categories and ideals, which was not really the case, according to Perniola.[8] When one now looks at how, for example, (high) art was classified in modernity, through the work of the picky taxonomists of the (mainly Western Central) European upper class (counting its diaspora and colonial outreach[9]), it really is not that much based on any reasonable way of discussing artistic work and aesthetic experience, as so much that is interesting and important is left out (aesthetic practices of females, workers, and other cultures).[10] The category is hard to see as having been strong in any other sense than the power structures legitimating it if one wants to follow Perniola here on aesthetics.

According to Perniola, the weakening itself of some powers of modernity was not the point. There were invisible potentials hidden in the messy historical situation that scholars aimed to target with their discourse on postmodernity, and they did not arise from our interpretation of modernity. They lured philosophers out of their modern role, or at least made possible a new form of philosophizing, if not immediately, than at least slowly and increasingly. How to make sense through philosophizing was gaining a new momentum. Perniola did not jump on the bandwagon of hermeneutics that had kept the two giants of the Turin school, Umberto Eco (who also wrote for Vattimo's and Rovatti's book) and Gianni Vattimo, busy for decades, as he saw focusing on interpretation as being too involved in spending time on the past. Neither did he join forces with the typical late–twentieth-century thinkers on media, who were, in the philosophically not as rigid work of Marshall McLuhan and the media-idealist work of Nicholas Negroponte and Jaron Lanier, working on visions for a future change of humankind through the development of media. He turned his gaze toward the more uncanny predecessors in the continental field, the philosophers of excess (Blanchot, Klossowski, Lacan, Bataille, Cioran, Shestov, and de Sade) and the cynics.[11]

There was a need to step into the dank side of culture and learn from it. His dank humanities (my expression) worked on fragments of culture, in a somewhat Benjaminian fashion. While dank has traditionally meant the moist and the sticky, the cold and damp (the wine cellar and the humid caves), it acquired in contemporary Internet language a new meaning, which embraced the sensually excessive, absurdist meme culture and all forms of (campy) rogue designs that played, consciously or not, with rude images and rude image quality and, for example, saturated colors and a sense of cold feeling. The concept, that I here apply to Perniola's work, is not just about what Perniola writes about media but also about his philosophical methodology. He aimed to give philosophers a chance to dive into the maelstrom of media fragments, to lose their human, control-driven agency, and to turn more into intellectual reaction machines. The cold touch of Internet culture that sometimes feels awkward and its arbitrary, illogical (in a different way than arbitrary and contradictory in poesy) nature with not just Googling surprises and algorithms has less philosophical rigor than the world guided by Enlightenment philosophers and museum directors, and we should be conscious enough to understand that in aiming too much to control we miss the nature of reality. At the same time, there has been a long tradition, where unlearning from the logical, polished forms of thinking toward not just the inspirationally illogical, but also toward the unpleasant, hidden sides of life, the sides that are hard if not impossible to grab and/or accept, has already provided a base for understanding how to cope with the new irregularities and the creepy side of the media era. In Perniola's case, though, this turn starts to happen practically already before the Internet era, in the video revolution, and this was a path that he aimed to follow with his philosophy.

Our daily experience and our ways of cultivating aesthetic experience have transgressed without doubt since the days when there were just a couple of national TV channels and one had to dive into shady shops to get beyond official culture. The potentials that lie beyond the controlled pleasures of modernity have, of course, also included certain interpretations and experiences of the body, which were often to become overshadowed in theoretical discourse by the development of new media and its new impulses for experiencing media extensions. For Perniola, some early twists in our identity and experience of the soma were taking shape already in the 1980s and 1990s with what he calls the "video-man."[12]

The video-man is not a new form of humanity, but a sort of insensitive mediatic expansion of sensing, which the excess and uncontrollability of already video rentals and the hustle with tapes brought long before what we call the new media. One could think that surveillance, bad quality B-films on the shelf, home videos and video art already produced the first line of dank experience, which the Internet just made bigger and a part of today's media habitat. It might have taken already some of the first steps on the way to our increasing way of sometimes feeling less human and more media, and/or tech, which in the end leads us to have experiences of ourselves as just tired machines or only things.[13] It might have awoken a bit some of those experiences we sometimes have now, when it feels that life is not just less in control in the maelstrom of smart phone use, Netflix "zipping" and PC windows (open like a set of playing cards), but that experience itself is less and less one's own, or just an extension of the media itself – with the dreams that feel like someone "directed" them, the hallucinatory daytime naps where mails keep coming (in David Lynch like daydreams) and the phantom sensation of the phone's buzz in the pocket (when it is not there). It feels sometimes like the machines, media and tech we live with have taken a step beyond the limits we used to think we had control of. These small twists that we are not yet maybe that happy to even recognize, and even less ready to digest, is something that Perniola went after. Meeting, digesting and analyzing our own quirky layers that our age stimulated became a philosophical project for him.

Thingness

To get into what Perniola did, one should maybe start from his idea of thingness. To do that I will dive into a strain of personal memories. At one point in my career, I emptied my head, which was too tired and full of theoretical work way too often, by jogging. The practice quickly became absolutely too excessive: I gained a long-lasting infection in my ankle, and I sought help from a doctor. I was still, at the time, one of those people who thought a lot about the holistic, organic nature of human beings – partly based on assumptions and ideals gained from yoga and humaniora – but my doctor was nothing like that. They were one of those machine-like, cold people, who really had a non-humane touch, and used to make people like me unhappy, resulting in outbursts like "doctors should gain more education on how to meet people and how to interact with them." And they treated me like a machine, an object and/or thing – not maybe on purpose, but it was just their lack of interaction skills, which made me feel that way. I felt, for a moment, barely human, when they "repaired" me, although their treatment was not in any way negative in atmosphere. They just in a sense fixed my body like a robot, and to take it further, it felt a bit like one robot repairing another. I am not talking about a clear experience of this, but a sort of marginal impulse, a margin of experience.

The way we sometimes become treated like objects or the way we experience it, is, of course, nothing new in philosophy and critical theory. But I had not understood how that could also be a pleasant experience. It might even had been that I felt a bit like a broken thing. I had worked too hard, and I woke up feeling that my brain was like an overheated machine. I was so tired I had some unwanted thoughts, which accentuated how it was not in my control. My sleep had become bad and I jogged to relax and empty my head – absolutely too much.

It might sound radical to stress the pleasant side of the cold experience of not really being only a human being, and it might, to some extent, crave certain privileges for one to be able to experience it, at least the way that I explain it here. But it is nothing new for our mind-body. As already discussed earlier in this book, when my partners have sometimes been just (eyes closed) using me for sexual gratification, or sometimes when I have felt that I am just a well-working part of a good team (in sport/work), I have felt the same, although, of course, with a very different accent on the experience. I have also been just a climbing tree for cats and a mattress for dogs. It is not always that bad to be a thing or an object for someone else. And neither is it bad when someone asks you to clean up and explains what to do, programs you through the routine, so that you for a moment lose yourself, become the extension of the person guiding you.

Doctors have many times repaired me, sewing the skin and injecting complicated modern medicine into my body. In gastroscopy I felt, for a moment, that I became one with the endoscope – the thin, flexible tube used to look inside the stomach. Dentists have built my teeth with plastic. I sometimes lose myself while I am jogging through geometric routes in the concrete jungle made out of cubes – and also this does not necessarily have to be just a bad experience.[14] Dancing to endless repetitious pop music in a club lit with cold blue lights or driving along motorways so that the car feels just like an extension of me and vice versa, are all experiences where humanity loses a bit to outer forces, machines, and just things, and the experience is not something that we would have been thinking much about, although it in many ways is quite central to today's experience.

This is, of course, not a call to forget the important work done by all the critical theorists who have been defending our humanity against unwanted thingness – from Laura Mulvey's (in this book already discussed) "Visual Pleasure and Narrative Cinema" (1975), which problematized the gender asymmetry in American film, where female bodies were construed to be things for the gazes of certain masculinities, to W.E.B. Du Bois's groundbreaking philosophical treatment of race, *The Souls of Black Folk* (1903), where Du Bois, *the* African American philosopher of his generation, aspired to explain in detail for the reader how African Americans were human beings who had a soul, not animals, nor just things to be used for the benefit of others.[15] We have, for obvious reasons – humankind has suffered a great deal – been forced to remind ourselves and others constantly about the way we are not just things, and this has, of course, broadened out to be something that we today explain about animals, too, how they are sensitive, soulful, and holistic creatures that should be treated with care.

If we aim – paradoxically here – for a more holistic truth, we should also cover, of course, the path opposite to this tradition and these problems. And it is here where the dank side comes through. In Perniola's path one could say that if ever, now it is important to study what it means to be a human being, from the point of view where the experience of not being really human starts. The poor and mistreated of this planet work with and through their bodies, favelas and dwelling in trash, selling organs and their bodies in bed, spending lives in sweatshops and streets, and the way the more privileged digitalized class of human beings in this world thrive wired, zipping media, networking with smart phones and other intelligent devices, is truly like a dystopic vision of the future from some science fiction film of the 1970s with a societal touch. In the light of this vision, it might even sound positive that at least the privileged are increasingly dominated and run by machines, tech and media, more than the absolutely non-privileged, although no revenge of this type will change anything like in a movie – and we have already pinpointed that there are unforeseen pleasures lying in this system, too.

The video-man, Perniola's vision of a new layer of tech and media-based humanity that we acquired in the 1980s and 1990s, might have started a new way of sensing, being and thinking, if not dominantly, then at least marginally. At the same time, aesthetics has become a mainstream aspect of life, not the theory, but the aesthetic itself, which lies everywhere, just one finger touch away, all the time. Perniola called the late post-war era the "bureaucratic era," and there art, artistry and aesthetics was still a marginal, quite formal practice. But the new era, which we entered sneakily, made these features dominant,[16] and the extension of sensing went out from sitting in soft couches and touching design objects, to increasingly stimulating media, which extended the whole concept of sense. As an ex-member of the Situationist International, Perniola was, of course, conscious of Guy Debord's visions in the 1950s and 1960s, that only images bind societies together anymore, but he went further with it, dropping vision out to be just one form of sensing and aesthetic quality of our everyday life, and accentuated sensing, also as a part of gazing.

In his book *Del sentire*, Perniola stresses the way the transformation explained earlier also makes us numb, in a way, destroying our sensitivity, like ideology makes theory stiff, into a kind of "sensology." Anyone who has spent too much time at the laptop and with the smart phone can recognize the dangers of repetition. Dankness takes over, to some extent, and this cold atmosphere is something we might feel challenging, and we might be fighting back by keeping no-media days.

Boredom and meaninglessness are surprisingly one of the end results of the tech and media development of our time.[17]

As "cool" and "high" show something about the cold and narrow nature of contemporary culture through their new centrality as aesthetic concepts,[18] the experience of being just (like) a thing drops out a vast plurality of traditions of discussing experiences of the self, which is endlessly provoked to react to short videos with car crashes, cats and/or sexual content on Instagram as much as fast-paced media on today's television.

The Philosopher as a New Intermediary

Perniola's philosophical aim was to come to terms with this by adopting a new way of writing and doing philosophy. The philosopher, with their long history of controlling thoughts, could ask if it was time to become "just" an intermediary, a theoretical and philosophical gateway for phenomena that could so find new smart expressions through their work.[19]

> "We have the steadily growing impression that a process of reciprocal osmosis has occurred between man and things, with the result that the former has become similar to the latter, while the latter have assumed increasingly human characteristics."[20]

Jean Baudrillard noted a long time ago already that images had marinated us so thoroughly that it was sometimes hard to understand what was vision without their dominance, without them being already in some sense a priori for gazing at the world,[21] and now we have to at least ask ourselves if the same type of thing could have happened with devices, things, consumer objects, tech and media.

Perniola reminds us that Hegel defined Egypt as the site of enigma. "In Egyptian culture, things have human faculties: to the statues of the gods, freed from the gaze of men, are ascribed the power to see the visitors to the temples; so-called Memnons, gigantic stone simulacra, ring out at sunrise; mummies are able to exercise every vital function."[22] Our situation might thus bear a similarity to the one that Hegel explains. Plato was once afraid of the way the arts can take possession of us.[23] But now the whole world of things and products might be challenging us in new ways related to Plato's fears. As we lose ourselves to some extent when we write ourselves into literature and work on poems and prose (as Barthes has it), becoming literature[24], we now dive so much into thingness in our lives that it might create similar experiences. In today's culture we are often both possessed and taken over by an atmosphere of indifference – as not just punk and metal music have shown.[25] Also, many sports aim for endurance and apathy through repetition and extreme feats (jogging, trekking). Even vital sports and sex become (dull) processes of endurance and apathy for many.[26]

If the sports mentioned here are about physical endurance and becoming a nearly indifferent moving body, of course, being the mediator for media, also, is increasingly a physical activity, one that calls for endurance. As already discussed earlier, films are also more somatic, Internet sites – from tabloids to social media – are full of material that should influence us and our bodies through a reaction more than a well-built experience, and even spending so much time with media today must affect our bodies somehow, not just the constant shocks ("look how a giant spider exuviates"), but also the constant bombarding of vision with environments that are built by us (Minecraft) or sailed through with the help of the vision machinery of a drone.

Luigi Pareyson, the "father" of the Torino school, and teacher of Gianni Vattimo, Umberto Eco and Mario Perniola, once wrote that, seriously taken, interpretation, true interpretation, happens only at the limits of what one can understand.[27] To gain this position, one cannot just stay distanced from everything, and in control, and this is how I read Perniola's call for action, to let loose, to lose control, to become oneself a mediator, driftwood with an antenna, in the maelstrom of today's world of tech, media and new arts, and to make sense of it without extending aspirations toward well-defined end results.

One might as well be happy with becoming one with the system, but also an interpreter or a translator, maybe scrivener in the sense Giorgio Agamben gives it in his text "Bartleby or Contingency."[28] The scrivener's role might be more than just copying and translating, as we know from religions, where countless scriveners have written down words by God(s). Not to lift the role of the philosopher too high, though – I think that there is a price to pay if we are not able to transcribe better what happens with tech and media these days, and although not all philosophy can be about becoming a mediator only for what surrounds us, it might be one role that we might assign ourselves. And, regarding the form: not only logical writing and articles and books as wholes are maybe what we should strive for, but also fragments, threads of thoughts, and maybe even working with the media itself to convey thoughts, might be increasingly the job for us to do in the future. In this sense, the philosopher might need to become something that some contemporary art is about today. According to Perniola art has traditionally fought to express reality less than truth/illusion, but lately, in a world where reality becomes easily overshadowed, the artist often wants to wake us up, provoke a real reaction.[29]

Back to it:

> "The philosopher is precisely someone who turns him- or herself into nothing in order to listen to the present and all its enigmas, the person who silences his or her own desires, his or her own untidy affections and his or her own deeply held opinions in order to avoid placing obstacles and misleading screens in the way of an understanding of history's manifestations."[30]

To be a philosopher in the way Perniola ascribes to it, one needs, supposedly, openly to become just a thing, to suppress rationalist narratives and argumentation (scientific rhetoric) for the sake of understanding through a more mimetic way of writing, like a machine trained to sense, to lose distance and to keep sensitivity awoken, inviting readers to see the enigma, the maelstrom of culture where we all swim (and some drown), and also help us all to see more of its uncanny darkness than we have been willing and able to before.

Conclusions

Mario Perniola's media philosophy accentuates the need to understand media not only by controlling it, but by becoming one with its sensibilities. The philosopher and/or scholar of media might sometimes need to quit analysis, and just aim to become one with the maelstrom that today's media is. As nobody today controls the production of media, there is no idea to read media landscapes like they would make sense. To lose intellectual control might be our new challenge, on the way to understanding media. But it might really reward us in the end.

Notes

1 Mario Perniola, *Enigmas: The Egyptian Moment in Society and Art* (London – New York: Verso, 1995), 43.
2 Chapter 2 in Richard Rorty, *On Philosophy and Philosophers: Unpublished Papers 1960–2000*, ed. W.P. Malecki and Chris Voparil (Cambridge: Cambridge University Press, 2020).

3 Richard Rorty, *On Philosophy and Philosophers.*
4 See chapter 1 of Rorty, *On Philosophy and Philosophers.* I am thankful to Wojciech Malecki for our dialogue on the topic.
5 Mario Perniola, *Disgusti: Le nuove tendenze estetiche* (Roma: Castelvecchi, 1998), 62.
6 Gianni Vattimo and Pier Aldo Rovatti, eds, *Pensiero debole* (Milano: Garzanti, 1983). Vattimo also wrote a book with Richard Rorty called *The Future of Religion* (New York: Columbia University Press, 2002), where these ideas gained a distinctive analysis.
7 Mario Perniola, *Enigmas*, 43.
8 See the dialogue in Gianni Vattimo, *Filosofia al presente* (Milano: Garzanti, 1990), 54–67.
9 For more on this expansion, see Max Ryynänen, *On the Philosophy of Central European Art.*
10 Ibid.
11 Perniola, *Disgusti*, 38.
12 Perniola, *Enigmas*, 27–30.
13 See chapter 4 of this book.
14 Ossi Naukkarinen has written about our need to vary our use of the environment. Jogging in a rough harbor area might be needed as much as jogging in parks and forests. See Ossi Naukkarinen, "The City, Sin, and Enjoyment," in *The City as Cultural Metaphor – Studies in Urban Aesthetics*, ed. Arto Haapala (Lahti: Institute of Applied Aesthetics, 1998), 26–37.
15 See Laura Mulvey, "Visual Pleasure and Narrative Cinema" and W.E.B. Du Bois, *The Soul of Black Folks* (New York: Dover Publications, 1994).
16 Mario Perniola, *Del sentire* (Turin: Einaudi, 1991).
17 For more of these thoughts, see also N. Gunder Hansen, "Interview med Mario Perniola," *Semiotik* 4 (1982): 83–94.
18 Mario Perniola, *Contro la comunicazione.*
19 Perniola, *Enigmas*, 43.
20 Perniola, *Enigmas*, 44.
21 See, for example, Jean Baudrillard, *Simulacra and Simulation* (Ann Arbor: University of Michigan Press, 1994).
22 Perniola, *Enigmas*, 45.
23 On ideas about artistic possession in the history of philosophy, see, for example, Shusterman, Richard. "Aesthetic Experience and the Powers of Possession." *Journal of Aesthetic Education* 53, no. 4, Winter 2019: 2–23.
24 Perniola, *Enigmas*, 45.
25 Perniola, *Enigmas*, 47.
26 Perniola, *Enigmas*, 47–49.
27 Peter Carravetta, "An Introduction to the Hermeneutics of Luigi Pareyson," *Differentia: Review of Italian Thought* 3, art. 2 (1989): 217.
28 Giorgio Agamben, *Potentialities: Collected Essays in Philosophy* (Stanford: Stanford University Press, 1999), Chapter 15.
29 Vattimo, *Filosofia al presente*, 59.
30 Perniola, *Enigmas*, 43.

90   *Disgust, the Inorganic, and the Enigmatic*

Bibliography

Agamben, Giorgio. *Potentialities: Collected Essays in Philosophy*. Stanford: Stanford University Press, 1999.

Baudrillard, Jean. *Simulacra and Simulation*. Ann Arbor: University of Michigan Press, 1994.

Carravetta, Peter. "An Introduction to the Hermeneutics of Luigi Pareyson." *Differentia: Review of Italian Thought* 3, art. 2 (1989): 217–241.

Du Bois, W.E.B. *The Soul of Black Folks*. New York: Dover Publications, 1994.

Hansen, N. Gunder. "Interview med Mario Perniola." *Semiotik* 4 (1982): 83–94.

Mulvey, Laura. "Visual Pleasure and Narrative Cinema." *Screen* 16, no. 3 (1976): 6–18.

Naukkarinen, Ossi. "The City, Sin, and Enjoyment." In *The City as Cultural Metaphor – Studies in Urban Aesthetics*, edited by Arto Haapala, 26–37. Lahti: Institute of Applied Aesthetics, 1998.

Perniola, Mario. *Del sentire*. Turin: Einaudi, 1991.

Perniola, Mario. *Enigmas: The Egyptian Moment in Society and Art* London – New York: Verso, 1995.

Perniola, Mario. *Disgusti: Le nuove tendenze estetiche*. Roma: Castelvecchi, 1998.

Perniola, Mario. *Contro comunicazione*. Torino: Einaudi, 2004.

Perniola, Mario. *Il Sex Appeal dell'inorganico*. Torino: Einaudi, 2004.

Rorty, Richard. *On Philosophy and Philosophers: Unpublished Papers 1960–2000*, edited by W.P. Malecki and Chris Voparil. Cambridge: Cambridge University Press, 2020.

Ryynänen, Max. *On The Philosophy of Central European Art: The History of an Institution and its Global Competitors*. Lanham: Lexington Books (an Imprint of Rowman and Littlefield), 2020.

Shusterman, Richard. "Aesthetic Experience and the Powers of Possession." *Journal of Aesthetic Education* 53, no. 4 (Winter 2019): 2–23.

Vattimo, Gianni, and Pier Aldo Rovatti. Eds, *Pensiero debole*. Milano: Garzanti, 1983.

Vattimo, Gianni. *Filosofia al presente*. Milano: Garzanti, 1990.

Vattimo, Gianni, and Richard Rorty. *The Future of Religion*. New York: Columbia University Press, 2002.

6 Rasafiction: Can the Oldest Atmosphere Theory in the World Help us to Understand Today's Somaesthetic Manipulation?

Snigdha Poonam's *Dreamers: How Young Indians Are Changing the World* (2018) reports on the growing ego, global aspirations and hybrid (Indian and post-colonial) culture of the youth of the largest middle class in the world. While we often think we are roaming on American webpages and clicking links offered by British clickbait companies, it is more often than we believe Indian companies, and their growing international work that we are looking at. It has just been offered to us like it has been produced by countries we feel more accustomed to.[1]

Having visited a couple of art and design universities in India and had the luck to teach some absolutely excellent Indian students, who, after finishing BAs in India set their target to become more international, I have noticed that mainly, in art schools and humanities, when students lay their hands on theory in India, it is Anglophile philosophy and theory, mainly British, that they read. One side path, though, exists: rasa theory. Developed first by the sage Bharata (500BC-500AD), then redeveloped most famously by the eleventh-century philosopher Abhinavagupta, it works on sentiments and/or emotional atmospheres.

As our digital age is increasingly Indian, and as I believe that we falsely believed in China's expansion to be the central country of the future – its (for the Westerners frightening) non-democratic nature and inability to find a common language with the West became obstacles – but that India might make it, following, for example, the greatest amount of people working in any country, its fluency with English (which is, according to Poonam, just increasing), and its somewhat sneaky investment in not just tech but also our everyday use of it, the fact that there here is another type of theoretical discourse, that most Indians who create our digital environments are somewhat aware of, raises questions. Although it is already a convention that I meet people

DOI: 10.4324/9781003248514-6

from China at conferences on humanities, who talk about Dao and Confucius, these world-views, alternative philosophies and ways of knowledge are not providing theories which would methodologically work as helpful in understanding the digital age. But rasa theory does it.

Just yesterday, I entered a mall. There was catchy and a bit sleazy background music that kept manipulating me while I walked through the long corridors with clothing shops and perfumeries, so that I'd make it to my grocery. Digital designs from logos to changing, turning, and moving images, and advertisements, kept my eyes semi-active all the way. It is quite the same in St. Petersburg, the Emirates and my hometown of Helsinki. On the underground, I read the news with my smart phone, my eyes dwelling on a pleasant, warm, and soft-coloured visual landscape – that an "inspirational speaker" I could not escape at a conference (in Bengaluru) once called the most valued real estate in the world. I send an SMS home – and the telephone, together with sign pads in the metro walls that share news and nice pictures from the readers, keep me slightly upbeat, and accentuate that I am in a "safe, smart city" and context. (Of course, siren servers keep on dragging me in to the Maelstrom of do-it-yourself media, too.[2]) If I have the sound on, my mobile keeps on beeping pleasantly, and if I drop in for a moment to do some social media, I am stimulated not just by friends' images on how many mushrooms they have picked and how many buns they have baked, but also other visuals and alluring links that take me, not coincidentally, to shaving machine pages and threads on funny looking terriers.

And working places start to resemble malls. My university's intranet pages already have so much upbeat spam that it is getting hard to find the facts I am after. And the corridors on the way to the lecture hall are filled with screens that, besides event information, accentuate the liberal, upbeat nature of my workplace, sometimes in an absurd way, like having pictures of professors saying that students should revolt to make a better world. Elevators play music. (That is no news anymore.) Our increasingly smart cars make pleasant sounds and blink lights, juicy green when there is enough gasoline, and nice, Star Wars-type electric sounds when you close the doors of the fanciest models.

It is not like in old films, when they attempt to understand what life in the future really is – like in Blade Runner, where an apocalyptic rain works side by side with massive, impressive moving images. Our everyday audiovisual stimulation is something else. It is an endless texture of small sounds, small lights, small images, often short in time, and transparent in our everyday – not really tools that we would not recognize, but supporters of a comfort zone where we feel safe and know where we are at. We are surrounded by a texture of small impulses. There are code colors: green and blue for meditative, pleasant, chilled out atmosphere – and red for warnings.

We have, of course, for a long time, historically, been supported by everyday design, from facades, decorations and details of architecture to city planning. Those who were richer have had at home everyday design from fancy sugar bowls to tapestries and even live musical performers as background music. Today we, an incredibly large amount of people, receive so much more sensual and/or aesthetic stimulation than ever, from professional designers, who, we could say, design quite a chunk of our lifeworld. The way our everyday is designed, from readymade food to dog breeds, clothes, teeth and cars, has acquired a new layer of holistic public space design and digital aesthetics. We ourselves take part in personalizing computers and smart phones, at least partly by making aesthetic decisions – but this is only the start: I recently visited a Tata car factory (in India), where they were working on cars with user IDs, so that when your partner stepped into the car, it would change the personalization.

How much do we yet understand this? At least, I have noticed, there are not really yet attempts to grab this from the point of view of critical theory – if one does not desire to think, for example, of Max Horkheimer's and Theodor Adorno's mimetic society dominated by the culture industry or Guy Debord's society of the spectacle, as early, dystopic guesses on where we might be going. I just, still, don't see the situation as that bad or totalitarian. Also, Adorno's main attack was on the authoritarian nature of culture, and he even asked for more dialogical nature from the media, considering the phone to be a better medium than the radio,[3] and Debord focused only on images, although today's world, which both feeds us and adjusts to us, is both visual and auditive, and in the future, one can guess, maybe it will also become olfactory, absolutely more robotized and definitely dialogical, maybe increasingly hacked into us. Media stalks us increasingly to get what we desire: not really what we really, really desire, but what we want from our close environs, and from the packages and everyday taxonomies it offers. And we take part in building the whole, actively.

As already said, when our everyday is artistically dramatized and intensified, many traces often lead to India. I already met the man who changed Jason Statham's face on the original footage onto stuntmen in a couple of films that I watched tired, after work – and for fun, he moved Statham's face around the screen for a while, laughing, with a latte in his hand. We were sitting deep in the incredible factory of *Lebenswelt*, Tata's headquarters in Bengaluru, where my host at the Sristhi college of art and design had taken me. The man was one of those millions who, in Snigdha Poonam's bestseller *Dreamers* (2018), work on our life worlds – without us realizing where our comfort comes from. *Dreamers* presents the growing profession of illusion-building. When we click on different feeds where we are presented with fun dog images and tests like "which character from Star Wars are you," we often somehow, maybe not intentionally, but still, think we dwell in a cultural landscape produced for us by our old, still often dominant, life designers in the United States, but actually, very often, we are comforted by the dreamers of India, who have cleverly become aware of how to stimulate us so that we feel our digital environment feels Western, that is, "normal."

Poonam, who worked for the Hindustan Times, was going to just make a short article about what young people in "small towns" want from life. She began from Ranchi, her hometown. The trip into the life of Generation Y extended into a 4-year book-writing process. She found a generation that wanted to conquer the world, and they worked through digitalization. They were anxious about their future, but they worked hard to make it globally. In 2020 India reached a nearly 900 million-strong working population, the largest in the world, and the young generation knows this. Why would not the world be run with their rules? Ambitions and crushing limitations of culture and society come together in these destinies. But they work hard to affect the world. They dream big. They are the "clickbaiters who create viral content for Facebook and the Internet scammers who stalk you at home," Poonam writes.

How can we cope with this digital development that I talked of? Not that naming India would immediately mean that its 1000- to 2000-year-old debates on aesthetics would mean anything anymore, but... as all these design school graduates know rasa theory, and, as it seems, they have a key role in the production of global everyday atmospheres, it might be plausible that rasa theory might be having an effect already through art and design education. Even more, it is the first atmosphere theory in the world. In a culture that is so massively stimulating sensually, India, it interestingly focuses on what happens only on stage (not in everyday culture) when one has a break from everyday routines. Still, some of the basic ideas expressed in it might mirror what happens today, as we are more than ever also on stage with our social media and work platforms. Looking at people's Facebook and Instagram feeds, it seems that quite many of us pose like film stars, and do things in a Riefenstahlian manner for the camera. When once we could just lean back in a chair, especially the COVID years have made us "flat," 2D, sitting in boxes in a view, that often has even been recorded – on Zoom, on Teams, on Skype... We are stalked, monitored, presented audiovisually... We might be both audience and actors, and at least one major chunk of people who produce our digitally intensified life have had a look or two at Bharata and Abhinavagupta, not Böhme, Sloterdijk or Griffero, the Western proponents of atmosphere theory. And, as rasa theory has also been the manual for the dramatic arts on the Indian continent for something like 2000 years (Bharata is the Aristotle of India, and even more), why would it not affect all Indian work on dramatization, also the dramatization of the everyday – at least a bit? It is important to note that rasa theory is not just having an impact in theory, but has a widespread impact on Indian arts and culture.

So why not dive into the rasa? And, why not ask what kind of a somatic effect these digital environments, and the atmospheres that we live in, have.

An idea history of the rasa:

Bharata's life project was to write about theater, the spectacles that were typical of the Indian continent. The *Nāṭyaśāstra* (*A Treatise on Dramatic Art*)[4] is as much a taxonomy as it is a DIY book, explaining everything in detail like the reader would be both a part of a growing, reflective audience, and someone who would be into directing plays. It includes everything imaginable from visuals to sound, from faces to colors used on stage.

As a pedagogical manual, the *Nāṭyaśāstra* has been incredibly influential in India, and this concerns not just the works of scholars, but the way makers of theater and dance spectacles, and artists of all type – in the twentieth century, film-makers – have been reading the book to come to terms with their art.

As the taxonomy is non-reflective, and talks about things on stage as clear facts, it makes one think that the original tradition that Bharata wrote about might have been very clearly coded. It is, of course, possible that it was not, and the early theorist here interpreted it in a too-simplified way, just creating a clean taxonomy which does not really tell us much about the work of art gazed upon, but at least like Aristotle's *Poetics*, which became both a descriptive and normative concept, and which so had a huge influence on, for example, seventeenth-century France,[5] the rasa theory of Bharata (and his followers) has since become present in such an amount of work on the Indian continent that it would be unrealistic to claim that one could not today, probably, find traces of it nearly everywhere where a professional dramatizes culture and/or the everyday somehow.

The book itself offers a possibility of an authority-driven reading, which is, of course, in unison with the Indian guru-tradition that has had an impact on the educational system of the culture. Bharata lists all kind of phenomena with pornographic detail. He talks, for example, about all the possible movements of the eye (36, all in all) – and explains how you can move your eyebrows (seven ways) and the significance of different ways of moving them.

In the long and rich thread of commentaries that this original text produced, rasa took sides with not just dramatic art, but also with poetry, painting, and music, blooming some centuries later through the work of a variety of authors (e.g. Bhatta Lollata, Shri Shankuka, Bhatta Nayaka, Ānandavardhana), who also enriched the original way of thinking with thoughts about the audience (Abhinavagupta) and the (quite somatic, it seems) bliss of rasa. The most modern philosophical view of all these classics is the *Abhinavabhāratī*, a commentary work written by the philosophical tantric, Abhinavagupta (c.950–1016).[6]

The main thing about the rasa, the theory of the emotive atmospheres and/or sentiments (there is no accurate translation into English), is the list of the eight rasas. Every possible theater piece has, according to the way of thinking, only one main rasa, and Bharata as much as the later commentators stress that this has to be chosen by the author – and, in many cases, consumed by a spiritually and aesthetically "woken" audience.

This is the atmospheric state we experience when we experience theater. It is not, though, the same thing as the sentiments and emotive atmospheres that dominate our everyday. Like the later paradox of fiction discussion in the modern West – why do we experience strong emotions when we watch Hamlet even if we know it is fiction?[7] – this theory, as early as two millennia ago, was already explaining the tension between the intellectual distance from fiction and the intimacy and our strong reactions we anyway gain with it. In the rasa version of this way of thinking, the *bhavas*, that is, the everyday mindset (emotions) form the psychological foundation of what happens on stage. What happens on stage uses these mindsets as the base for the sentiments and/or atmospheres produced in theater. Sucharita Gamlath explains this as being actually a *reduced version* of the emotion, represented and expressed.[8] It still possesses the viewer, maybe even in a more intensive manner than in our everyday life, but it is another version of the same basic type of experience. As John Dewey writes that an aesthetic experience ("an experience," in Dewey's words) gathers our memories and other experiential resources together and intensifies our experiential state,[9] the early rasa theorists – the first to come up with an extensive theory of aesthetic experience! – explain that these resources, actual memories and lived experiences, become material for the stage version, where the authors of the play together with the audience elevate them into a more spiritual, and, most importantly, into a more reflective experience. Through aesthetic sublimation happens something that is typical of religious experiences, a topic of discussion which has been even more dominant in Indian philosophy.

In Abhinavagupta's sense-sensitive interpretation of the rasa, sight and hearing are addressed as the strongest senses. Only they, when used in the right way, are able to drive us out of our everyday shell (my expression) into this parallel world, the heightened sense of thinking and experiencing, that the rasa, like any religious ecstasy makes possible. During a performance one entered "another world, in some measure an unreal one, and" lost oneself "in it completely."[10] This does not naturally sound that much like the culture we have fostered as highbrow, from museums to intellectual performances and complex, slow films like Andrey Tarkovsky's, which crave intellectual reflection. We have mostly, in the West, stressed that losing oneself (through becoming absorbed in the work), that is, "aesthetic self-forgetfulness," belongs to the uncritical consumption of popular culture[11]. As Arindam Chakrabarti writes, the experience discussed by rasa theorists, though, comes close to the English language concepts "amazing" and "awesome."[12] This sounds more like pop music and Netflix than Beckett or even bourgeois plays. The experience lifts the viewer somehow out from their everyday position and makes everything distanced, and possible to be reflected on. It overcomes the ego in this remarkable win for arts and culture in classical Sanskrit thinking, which mostly stressed just religious experience. Aestheticized emotions take over and overshadow everyday emotions.[13] It is a meta-feeling, which uses as ingredients everyday feelings – and a sort of universal structure that one enters, leaving one's self behind.[14] Still, it hits us – strongly.

The Erotic (*Śṛṅgāra*), the Heroic (*Vīra*), Terror (*Raudra*), Disgust (*Bībhatsa*), the Humorous (*Hāsya*), Compassion (or Pathos, *Karuṇa*), Wonder (or Magical, *Adbhuta*) and Dread (*Bhayānaka*)[15] all have their own code colors and rules for conduct on stage. They are "the cumulative result of stimulus, involuntary reaction and voluntary reaction," as Bharata writes.[16]

Good artists are able to use the everyday resources that people have as ingredients for the *rasa*. They kind of squeeze out a juice from these existing memories and everyday sentiments, which lose their individual nature, and become one – like a sauce which uses different herbs, and in the end has "just" a rich taste. This "flavor," which at the same time is a state of reflection, wonder, and bliss, although stimulated by the basic senses, reaches in the end beyond the senses, and helps the audience to get beyond their "selves," submerged in the play and its world, experiencing not their own but "any" emotions, emotions on an abstract level. Still, the experience described is far from the Western highbrow one, which is, for example, nearly always disinterested, detached, and intellectual to some extent. This is intensive and strong, as said.

While modern and/or contemporary writings on *rasa*, however excellent they might be, mostly work on canonizing the classics and doing exegetic research on the tradition, not much has been done to discuss the possible applications of *rasa* theory today. There are some texts about film and some notions on TV series and contemporary culture[17], but we are still lacking a view on our culture as a whole, which would be as holistically portrayed as it was done in the old *rasa* theories, where the everyday was always an important part of the theorized topic. While the original theorists focus mainly on theater or some other "awesome" moments of artistic work or consumption, there is no longer any reason to narrow the discourse down to only these moments. Of course, one could think of the rich cultural tradition of India, which might be one of the most shockingly holistic sense-wise with all of its scents, colors and audiovisual treats, and say that the ancients could have always applied rasa theory to their everyday. Still, there's a long way to go from eleventh-century Kashmir to, for example, today's middle-class Helsinki, where I sit, in the basement of my house, writing this chapter – right now my eyes only turned toward the PC, but later reading Proust, watching Netflix, listening to music with my daughter and spending time in a home designed by professionals in graphics and design who made our sofas, shelves and TVs, without forgetting book covers and the whole town planning outside of my window. Professional world-making is wider and deeper than ever, and the way it builds our experience, especially in the digital world, has taken incredible steps during even just recent decades. It is not that I'd feel, after watching *Narcos* or going through my daily social media, a "higher Shakti," a "capacity of awareness of the self," as G.T. Deshpande expresses one of *rasa*'s impacts,[18] although one can say that sometimes, of course; with the complicated network of stimulation offered by smart phones, advertising, and contemporary popular culture, one can also gain a sense of second-level reflection (we are often surrounded by really witty adverts and educationally genius infotainment). Mainly, though, certain atmospheres, sentiments are marinating me for long periods – like on my trip to the mall, which I already described briefly at the beginning of this chapter. It might not be that I could talk about "disgust" or "the erotic," two important rasas from the list, but definitely the atmospheres of digital culture, its virtual office spaces as much as its DIY human resources (like Facebook, Instagram, and Twitter), bring about something that could be called *rasa*, too. They might stress efficiency, like my digital PC environment with its audio signals and often gray, shallowly colorful frames offered for my work. If we put aside for a moment the fact that *rasa* in classical Indian theater is something different from these professionally made, aesthetic atmospheric phenomena that I am here writing about, we all recognize the PC work *rasa* and the social media *rasa* that make us feel uplifted, connected to certain practices and communities.

One cannot say there is anything spiritual at stake here, but on the other hand, do we, readers of today – me not, at least – believe that theater in Abhinavagupta's or Bharata's time really elevated people to a universal divine plane, or would it seem more fit in this case to think of this the same way as we now, with profane distance, read Plato and his conceptions of the world of ideas? There was no art system in Sanskrit times and it probably felt natural to discuss the bliss that sometimes happened when one was following artistic work in awe through religion. And, thinking about the bliss, the moment when the work really caught us, the original *rasa* theorists did not discuss in any way the need to look at whole art works, which in the end is a very late-Western feature of art theories, mainly modernist ones, where the whole, the "work" as a whole, became important to always note when discussing details during the eighteenth and nineteenth centuries.[19] Why not, then, talk about the moments when our egos are somewhat overcome and/or overshadowed, for example, when thrills pass our eyes and ears, from cats on Instagram to raunchy tabloid webpages and to the first beats of a new rap piece and its vicious video. We do not necessarily need to think of immersion into works of art. We are surrounded by textures and details that invade our experience, producing sometimes awe, although often just a sort of atmospheric feeling. While provoking disgust, for example, might be an easy way to overcome our intentional states with a reaction, that takes over our phenomenological field, as Aurel Kolnai was already writing in the 1930s,[20] we are softly seduced to take up consumerist atmospheres and light-hearted, pleasure-driven atmospheres, sometimes extensively throughout our everyday lives. We do not need to lose ourselves completely in the way an intensive play makes us. It can happen in a soft way, during the day, while we do not really notice it, and just a bit, when the sentiment takes over. There are levels of emotive atmosphere. Some can be strong, some weak. And most of today's commercial and/or upbeat commercial sentiments are a bit like background music. We dwell in them without noticing it.

And, as India keeps producing the people who keep producing the atmospheres where we are, increasingly, and effectively, they come up with the *rasa* for us – nerds in Mumbai, Delhi, and Bengaluru, maybe not that different from the nerds in California, Finland or China, but still with knowledge of the ancient ways of thought discussed here, through education in design schools, and through inhaling it every-where in Indian culture. These professionals, wherever they come from, build our sentiments, to some extent. They build the "half-things," as Tonino Griffero calls atmospheres,[21] which accompany us, and so we experience their products, the sentiments driven by designn and bombard through endless digital distribution – and which thus are not, like the original *rasa* are not, our own experiences, but products in themselves, readymade atmospheres, where we easily fit in.

Rasafication has become bigger and bigger, and we need to stop and look around us, to really grab the issue. How much are you today stimulated by readymade atmospheres, by networks of textures pro-duced by big companies, which affect your moods – consciously or unconsciously?

Abhinavagupta writes: "let us revert to the spectator. His own self continues to be merged in the represented exploits, and through it, he goes on seeing everything in this light.[22]" Does not that, also, sound familiar? And this play we are all in, on a daily basis. This *Gesamtkunstwerk* is the contemporary life form that we live in, our habitat. We already know that pop music is the "soundtrack of our lives." There is just so much more to it.

And if the bliss is sometimes somatic, making us blush a bit (while walking by the lingerie shop and its smooth audiovisual screenings), forcing us to feel the bass of the music playing in the clothing shop, raising romantic feelings or a feeling of warmth for seasonal reasons (when we see Christmas decorations, for example), and, to not forget this, just feel comfortable in our bodies when we are surrounded by the right products, the right digital audios, soft colors and the icons that we are used to, there is also another side to it. Our endless return to wired culture – many feel that this is an addiction they need to work on – which fragments our everyday experience, makes us jump into the nasty looking tabloid pages every hour, and to react to mails that pop up in the upper part of the screen when we are attempting to concentrate on writing, making our bodies nervous, in a way that no laid-back design can in the end help us with. This is maybe the final *rasa* to look at: the way the devices we use irritate our brains and bodies, make our thighs feel like the phone is vibrating ("is someone calling me?"), and how it captures our imagination, makes people desire to operate their body (as they have gazed at the flow of "perfect" bodies on Instagram), or to mimic other things seen, from make up to the way of walking some social media stars make (in)famous. This is the somatic rasa of our time. This is the final atmosphere which we know from extensive media use, the one where our body is alert all the time, feeling hectic and irritated. This rasa dominates our somatic lives, and we all take part in creating it, and accepting it – a daily body terror, where the body does not gain much peace. It is an offspring that lives its own life, maybe forever in our bodies, which are ready to jump up and gaze at a possible SMS coming up, even years after all this is gone, and other digital cultures (and whatever comes after them) are dominating our everyday.

Conclusions

India's cultural role is growing. If Aristotle was used to explain Hollywood movies, which dominated many of us totally still in the end of the twentieth century, do we now need Indian thinking to help us to understand where we are at? The ancient rasa theory, which focuses on atmospheres/sentiments, has an impact on all Indian arts, not just historically, but today too. Discussing today's digital manipulation with the help of rasa theory, for sure, gives us many perspectives which we have not had before. We live, more than ever, in readymade atmospheres created by designers. How can we cope with this change? Although the study here does not give plain answers, I hope it has been able to shed some light on the complex issue, which is a part of today's cultural situation, where we find ourselves in.

Notes

1 Snigdha Poonam, *Dreamers: How Young Indians Are Changing The World* (London: C. Hurst & Co., 2018).

2 Jaron Lanier uses this term about, for example, Youtube: Jaron Lanier, *Who Owns the Future* (New York: Simon & Schuster, 2013).

3 The telephone "still allowed the subscriber to play the role of subject, and was liberal" – referred to radio. Adorno and Horkheimer, "Culture Industry," 42.

4 Bharata Muni, *The Nāṭyaśāstra: English Translation with Critical Notes* (New Delhi: Munshiram Manoharlal Publishers, 1984). See also, for example, *The Bloomsbury Research Handbook of Indian Aesthetics and the Philosophy of Art*, ed. Arindam Chakrabarti, 149–166 (London: Bloomsbury, 2016). For Abhinavagupta's rasa theory, see Romano Gnoli's translation with notes: Romano Gnoli, *The Aesthetic Experience According to Abhinavagupta* (Varanasi: Chowkhamba Sanskrit Series Office, 1956).

5 See, for example, Klaas Tindeman's "The Politics of the Poetics: Aristotle and Drama Theory in seventeenth century France," *Foundations of Science* 13, no. 3 (2008): 325–333.

6 For an overview, read, for example, *A Rasa Reader: Classical Indian Aesthetics*, ed. Sheldon Pollock (New York: Columbia University Press, 2016).

7 See, for example, Eva-Maria Konrad, Thomas Petraschka and Christiana Werner, "The Paradox of Fiction – A Brief Introduction into Recent Developments, Open Questions, and Current Areas of Research, including a Comprehensive Bibliography from 1975 to 2018," *Journal of Literary Theory* 12, no. 2 (2018): 193–203.

8 Sucharita Gamlath, "Indian Aesthetics and the Nature of Dramatic Emotions," *British Journal of Aesthetics* 9, no. 4 (1969): 372–386. Note on page 372.

9 John Dewey, *Art as Experience* (New York: Perigee Books, 1980).

10 Sheldon Pollock, "Introduction," *A Rasa Reader: Classical Indian Aesthetics* (New York: Columbia University Press, 2016), 1.

11 For an overview, see, for example, Richard Shusterman, *Pragmatist Aesthetics*.

12 Arindam Chakrabarti, "Introduction," in *The Bloomsbury Research Handbook of Indian Aesthetics and the Philosophy of Art*, ed. Arindam Chakrabarti (London: Bloomsbury, 2016), 1.

13 Chantal Maillard, "What is Meant by 'Art' in India – Western Misunderstandings," in *Asian Aesthetics*, ed. Ken-ichi Sasaki (Singapore: NUS, 2010), 190.

14 Arindam Chakrabarti, "Ownerless Emotions in Rasa-Aesthetics," in *Asian Aesthetics*, ed. Ken-ichi Sasaki (Singapore: NUS, 2010), 198.

15 Bharata, *The Nāṭyaśāstra*, 56.

16 Ibid., 55.

17 See, for example, Max Ryynänen, "Rasa Industry."

18 G.T. Deshpande, *Abhinavagupta* (Mumbai: Sahitya Akademi, 1989), 78.

19 See, for example, Lydia Goehr, *Imaginary Museums of Musical Work*, 8.

20 Kolnai, "Disgust."

21 Tonino Griffero, *Atmosferologia: Estetica degli spazi emocionali* (Roma-Bari: Laterza, 2010).

22 Gnoli, *The Aesthetic Experience According to Abhinavagupta*, 97.

Bibliography

Adorno, Theodor, and Max Horkheimer. "Culture Industry: Enlightenment as Mass Deception." In *Dialectics of Enlightenment: Philosophical Fragments*, 94–136. Stanford: Stanford University Press, 2002.

Chakrabarti, Arindam. "Ownerless Emotions in Rasa-Aesthetics." In *Asian Aesthetics*, edited by Ken-ichi Sasaki, 197–209. Singapore: NUS, 2010.

Chakrabarti, Arindam. "Introduction." In *The Bloomsbury Research Handbook of Indian Aesthetics and the Philosophy of Art*, edited by Arindam Chakrabarti, 1–24. London: Bloomsbury, 2016.

Deshpande, G.T. *Abhinavagupta*. Mumbai: Sahitya Akademi, 1989.

Dewey, John. *Art as Experience*. New York: Pedigree Books, 1980.

Gamlath, Sucharita. "Indian Aesthetics and the Nature of Dramatic Emotions." *British Journal of Aesthetics* 9, no. 4 (1969): 372–386.

Gnoli, Raniero. *The Aesthetic Experience According to Abhinavagupta*. Varanasi: Chowkhamba Sanskrit Series, 1956.

Griffero, Tonino. *Atmosferologia: Estetica degli spazi emozionali*. Roma-Bari: Laterza, 2010.

Kolnai, Aurel. "Disgust." In *On Disgust: Edited and with an Introduction by Barry Smith and Carolyn Korsmeyer*. Chicago: Open Court, 2004.

Lanier, Jaron. *Who Owns the Future*. New York: Simon & Shuster, 2013.

Maillard, Chantal. "What is Meant by 'Art' in India – Western Misunderstandings." In *Asian Aesthetics*, edited by Ken-ichi Sasaki, 188–196. Singapore: NUS, 2010.

Muni, Bharata. *The Nāṭyaśāstra: English Translation with Critical Notes*. New Delhi: Munshiram Manoharlal Publishers, 1984.

Pollock, Sheldon. Ed. *A Rasa Reader: Classical Indian Aesthetics*. New York: Columbia University Press, 2016.

Poonam, Snigdha. *Dreamers: How Young Indians Are Changing The World*. London: C. Hurst & Co., 2018.

Ryynänen, Max. "Rasa Industry." In *Aesthetics in Dialogue: Applying Philosophy in a Global World*, edited by Zoltan Somhegyi and Max Ryynänen, 95–106. Berlin: Peter Lang, 2020.

Shusterman, Richard. *Pragmatist Aesthetics: Living Beauty, Rethinking Art*. London: Blackwell, 1992.

Tindeman, Klaas. "The Politics of the Poetics: Aristotle and Drama Theory in 17th Century France." *Foundations of Science* 13, no. 3 (2008): 325–333.

Index

For Product Safety Concerns and Information please contact our EU representative GPSR@taylorandfrancis.com
Taylor & Francis Verlag GmbH, Kaufingerstraße 24, 80331 München, Germany